WHY THERAPISTS CHOOSE TO BECOME THERAPISTS

Other titles in the UKCP Series:

WHY THERAPISTS CHOOSE TO BECOME THERAPISTS

A Practice-Based Enquiry

Sofie Bager-Charleson

On behalf of the United Kingdom Council
for Psychotherapy

KARNAC

First published in 2010 by
Karnac Books Ltd
118 Finchley Road, London NW3 5HT

British Library Cataloguing in Publication Data

A C.I.P. for this book is available from the British Library

ISBN: 978 1 85575 826 1

Edited, designed and produced by The Studio Publishing Services Ltd
www.publishingservicesuk.co.uk
e-mail: studio@publishingservicesuk.co.uk

www.karnacbooks.com

CONTENTS

ACKNOWLEDGEMENTS

This book is written together with members of the Reflective Writing Group. Thank you colleagues and co-authors: Pamela Critchley, Sherna Ghyara Chatterjee, Sheila Lauchlan, Susan McGrath and Francesca Thorpe. Without your experience, wisdom, and insightful reflections this book would not exist.

Sofie Bager-Charleson is an integrative psychotherapist and super-visor. She works with individuals and couples, with a special inter-est in relationship patterns and communication. She holds a PhD from Lund University in Sweden, where she specialized in attach-ment issues within families and reflective practice among teachers. She is a writer of both fiction and non-fiction. She works as an aca-demic adviser for psychotherapists on the work-based doctorate programme, DPsych, with Metanoia/Middlesex University. She runs workshops and courses in creative and reflective writing, in Sweden and England. Sofie is the editor of the book, and has writ-ten Chapters One–Four and Ten.

Sherna Ghyara Chatterjee, MA in Psychoanalytic Psychotherapy and Diploma in Integrative Counselling, with over sixteen years' experience in private practice. Sherna works with individuals and couples for short-term and long-term psychotherapy. Sherna also works in the NHS. Her special interest remains applying psycho-therapy across different cultures. She divides her time between India and the UK. Sherna has authored Chapter Seven, where she writes about why she chooses to work in intercultural psychotherapy.

Pamela Critchley, MSc, is an integrative psychotherapist. She works in private practice in Guildford, Surrey. Prior to training and working as a psychotherapist, she taught in schools, where she specialized in working with special needs children within the mainstream system. After a break to have a family, she lectured in child development at Guildford College. Pam writes Chapter Nine in the book, where she shares the result of her research and muses on the theme of why she is a therapist.

Sheila Lauchlan, MSc, is a systemic psychotherapist who works with couples, families, and adolescents. She focuses on repetitive communication patterns and their effect on relationships. Sheila specializes in work with adults who have been sexually abused in childhood. She has researched the effects on men who have been abused by women in their childhood. Sheila worked as a mental health social worker for many years. She was encouraged to train as a psychotherapist. Once qualified, she worked as a university counsellor and as a therapist in a child and adolescent mental health team. She now works in private practice in Surrey. Sheila is the author of Chapter Five, where she writes about why she became a systemic psychotherapist.

Susan McGrath is a qualified psychosynthesis psychotherapist, with further training with Relate and the Westminster Pastoral Foundation. She works as a university counsellor in Surrey, where she runs groups for staff and students and offers both individual and couple counselling. Susan comes from Scotland. She spent five years in Tokyo, Japan, before she settled in the South of England with a small private practice and her work at the student counselling service. Susan is the author of Chapter Eight, where she reflects over her motivations for working as a transpersonal therapist.

Francesca Thorpe works as a school counsellor and an integrative counsellor in Surrey. Prior to this, she worked as a registered general nurse, specializing in diabetes, in London. She has lived in Sydney and run a ceramic painting business before she embarked on the couples Relate training, followed by an individual BACP Accredited Three-Year Diploma in Integrative Counselling.

Francesca has worked as a counsellor for Relate, at a GP Surgery, for a Surrey-based charity, and at Kingston University. She now works as a school counsellor and has a small private practice at home. She works with couples, individuals, and adolescents, and specializes in working with disability issues, those connected with Thalidomide included. Francesca has written Chapter Six, where she reflects on how she works as an existentially informed therapist.

Introduction

Almost two decades ago, the psychoanalyst Sussman concluded that the therapist's motivation for practising was a neglected area. Is this perhaps a question best left alone?

> *"Perhaps therapists' motivations have been neglected for a good reason.* Do they really matter? *One could certainly argue, for instance, that automobile mechanics do not need to know why they chose to fix cars* for a living in order to perform adequately. Why should psychotherapists be any different? Well, to begin, *humans are far more complicated than cars,* and human interactions can be exceedingly complicated and multifaceted. Secondly, *introspection is unlikely to provide mechanics with greater understanding of motor vehicles . . .* A third distinction is that the therapist generally uses no mechanical instruments, no technology. *It is the person of the therapist that constitutes his or her primary tool.* [Sussman, 1992, p. 5, my italics]

This book revisits the questions raised above. We support Sussman's rationale for raising the issue in the first place and wonder if much has changed since he referred to it as a "neglected" area twenty years ago.

What brings us here?

This is an enquiry that moves from personal musing to collaborative and systematic inquiry. At the heart of the book lie six separate accounts, as told by counsellors and psychotherapists in a reflective writing and peer support group. Each therapist represents a different modality, and all come from very different backgrounds. These accounts are put into the context of ongoing literature and viewed with reference to a survey in which 238 other therapists provide their perspective on the question. As in the case of, for instance, Feltham (1999), Rowan and Jacobs (2003), and Wosket (2003, p. xi) "the therapist's use of self", is a key theme. It is particularly so in the case of Wosket, who approaches the area of the therapist's use of self with an interest in reflective practice. The attention paid to what therapists bring into the therapeutic relationship is shared with Page (1999), who explores the therapists' input in terms of both potential enlightenment *and* shadows.

For an in-depth account of the development in the therapeutic use of self on a more general basis, Wosket is, thus, particularly recommended reading. However, like Feltham, Rowan and Jacobs, and Page, Wosket focuses on *how* to practise. Our interest revolves around *why*. Why do we practise therapeutically in the first place? *What*, as Sussman (1992, p. 259) puts it, *"brings us here?"*

Depending on what basic belief we hold about reality, we refer to different sets of "truths" and generate certain kinds of knowledge. This book shares the belief, addressed by, for instance, Safran and Muran (2003), that *both* therapist and client are "constrained by preconceptions and prejudices" when they perceive "reality" and negotiate the therapeutic relationship. The reflective practice approach rests on the belief that all our understanding takes place through "framings". There is no way, argues Schön, the "father" of reflective practice, that we can make sense of social reality without selecting information in ways influenced by our own personal and cultural biases.

The reflective practice approach also offers an integrative framework for practitioners within the "helping professions" in general, which has been a relevant angle for us and our question, "why do some make 'helping others' into a profession?"

Reflective practice requires attention to the way in which we process information and new experiences. The book is, in this sense, an extension of a previous project about reflective practice within health and social care professions. It can be read alone, or in connection with the book titled *Reflective Practice in Counselling and Psychotherapy* (Bager-Charleson, 2010). A distinct theme in both these books is that some professions, more than others, rely on "judgements" coloured by personal, cultural, and theoretical values and beliefs. Reflective practice and reflexivity involves owning one's questions rather than relying on others to "carry" them for us. With this in mind, the author and the contributors of this book also have to "own up" to their interest in the matter. Why is choosing therapy as a profession an issue for us? We start by introducing ourselves.

"Owning" the question

Although labelled "peer supervision group", the group that evolved into our "reflective writing group" was always explicitly intended to nourish us, the practitioners. We knew each other well enough to recognize that this was, perhaps, what we, in spite of all our personal therapy and lengthy training, still found most difficult to commit to. Some of us have known each other since the beginning of our training. A few of us have been in training together, at different stages. We have seen each other embark on what actually surprised us all, a long, cumbersome, and expensive journey towards accreditation. We revealed hopes and dreams for each other before the training, which were revisited and sometimes re-evaluated at the end of it. We saw each other struggle with babysitting to volunteer in obscure outposts with sometimes neither heating nor appropriate security. We have struggled with essays together, cried, and sometimes sworn, over experiential groups at college and university; we have celebrated achievements and witnessed each other setting up private practices and assume our respective part- or full-time employment in different kinds of agencies. When we qualified, BACP and UKCP registered counsellors and psychotherapists agreed on the peer supervision group. In the first place, we felt qualified to support each other and trusting enough to address vulnerabilities and needs.

An ongoing theme, to be supported by each other, was to channel our energy in directions which responded to our "true" selves;

we wanted to have fun, agreed to be creative, and allow for plenty of space to make mistakes.

Many counsellors and psychotherapists will know that this kind of *overt* self-indulgence comes at a cost. Together with nurses, social workers, and others within what Guggenbuhl-Craig (1991) refers to as "ministering professions", therapists run a high risk of falling into the category of "compulsive helpers". A nice way of putting this stance is to describe therapists as helpful, empathic, and possibly wounded, but in the most selfless meaning of the word. As we shall see further on, less flattering angles to helpfulness are offered by Sussman (1992), Guggenbuhl-Craig (1991), and Miller (1997). They highlight how "helping" often is a way for the "narcissistically damaged" (Miller, 1997) to feed fantasies of "omnipotence, grandiosity and perfection" (Sussman, 1992, p. 110). Sussman writes,

> for many therapists, an attitude of benevolence constitutes an important feature of their ego-ideal ... Left unanalyzed, however, it can contribute to a significant "blind spot" ... The striving for an idealized, all-good image again recalls the myth of Narcissus ... *Omniscience, omnipotence and benevolence* are, in this sense three common components of broader aspiration—the *attainment of perfection. There are indications that, for many therapists, such an ambition predates their choice of profession.* [*ibid.,* pp. 118–119]

Why now?

Apart from expecting our clients to consider the question "what brings you here?", it is also customary to consider the clients' attendance in terms of "why now?"

As the co-ordinator and the main author of the book, I will have to pay careful attention not to disown my questions and project them upon you, the reader, or my friends and co-authors. I will often write in plural, referring to us and we, in the book. This is a result of the fact that all texts have been read and discussed within the group. The aim of our peer group has always been to encourage each other to develop previously neglected aspects of each other. In my case, writing is an interest which has flourished and developed during the project. By the time we agreed to incorporate

writing in our peer supervision group, I was in the process of publishing my first novel and had just started a course in teaching creative writing.

Others in the group have developed other dormant interests
during our peer group and the subsequent reflective writing.
Francesca, for example, in the aftermath of this project, has been
involved in an international pilot project for counselling of clients
who are victims of the drug Thalidomide. Sherna is embarking on
a specific writing project in intercultural therapy. Perhaps most
importantly, we have enjoyed ourselves during our writing and,
sometimes, late-night discussions.

Writing our separate stories has, in this sense, brought changes
on both a personal and professional level. This is something that
reflective learning and the process of investing in a reflexive awareness tends to do; it encourages us to reassess what we do and will
often trigger radical changes.

To me, a particular trigger for this project was the time when
Susan brought an article with her to one of our meetings. It was an
article about "Risk assessment: the personal safety of the counsellor" (Despenser, 2007). The article raised among us both concerns
and memories about our risk taking. Several of us had practised,
unpaid, in outposts which, at times, failed with regard to safety.
One of us recalled counselling a male client with anger management as his presented problem in a badly-lit outpost located along
a country lane. The usual secretary had failed to turn up, and
although the policy of the agency was not to practise unsupervised,
the idea of turning away the client was dismissed by my friend. She
said, "I didn't even think it was an option to turn him away. Why
didn't I? Perhaps it felt more provocative in itself to do so. I just
remember thinking in the middle of the session that no one will
hear me if anything happens to me. And I remember thinking, why
did I do this to myself?"

The moment in question was a turning point for my friend; she
spent considerable time in personal therapy to explore underlying
motifs for such "unselfish" self-destruction. Some of us in the group
share childhood issues, albeit of different kind. On one level or
another, however, we were all able to relate to the hypothesis in the
article that our own "grandiosity" puts both ourselves and our
clients at risk. Despenser (*ibid.*, p. 15) suggests that "a transference

infused with flattery and idealisation fuels the therapist's grandiosity and self-deception, and reinforces denial of risk".

As Miller concludes, grandiosity has actually very little to do with grandeur. It is, rather, categorized by an ongoing attempt to escape our "cut off, unloved self", which has had to give way to a "false" self.

The flip side of the coin, suggesting a need to save the world, is the unflattering assumption that we actually think that we *can* save the world. This usually unconscious underlying belief is, argues Guggenbuhl-Craig, the greatest trap for professional within the "ministering profession". The lengthy training on most therapy courses usually secures personal therapy. Sussman (1992) emphasizes that "it is also important that trainees gain an understanding of their dispositional tendencies as helpers, and to learn how to compensate for these proclivities". Long-term arrangements are required for this "ongoing" work with our shadow, as Guggenbuhl-Craig proposes:

> The future analyst becomes conscious of his shadow during the course of a good training and control analysis . . . An honest analyst will realise with horror from time to time that in his daily work he has been acting exactly like an unconscious quack and false prophet. [1992, p. 113]

Writing a book will perhaps sound just as deluded, compulsive, and grandiose as taking on potentially dangerous clients in unpaid, unheated agency outposts. Those who enjoy writing as much as we do will, however, recognize the immense joy which comes with this particular creative medium. Kottler (1993) writes about the importance of creative outlets; he regards them as safeguards against burnout. Many authors address the danger of relying on the client for a "life" (Fromm, 1998, p. 259), and personal enjoyment has been a priority for us in this project. Naturally, personal therapy and supervision are the first, most obvious resources to access by counsellors and psychotherapists in need of exploring their motives. This book has, however, grown in response to a need for complementary means to address work-related issues. and we have experienced peer support and creativity as important additional means for rejuvenation, on both a personal and professional level.

I think it is fair to say that this book was born out of a joint attempt to "own" our respective shadows. Not in order to be grandiose and unselfishly helpful, but simply because we have become aware of needing it for ourselves, and have assumed that others would benefit from this stance, indirectly. As Guggenbuhl-Craig (1992, p. 16) puts it, "We of the ministering professionals shall not be delivered from evil. But we can learn to deal with it".

Through reflective writing in a collaboratively run peer group, we have, in this sense, attempted to own our shadows rather than escape or disown them. Hawkins and Shohet iterate the issue in a way that resonates with many of us in the group:

> We believe that it is essential for all those in the helping professions to honestly reflect on the complex mixture of motives that have led them to choose their current profession and role . . . Aware of what Jungians call our "shadow" side, we will have less need to make others into the parts of ourselves that we cannot accept. [2008, p. 9]

Sussman (1992, p. 259) refers to Freud's analogies about the therapist as a mirror, blank screen, or surgeon as "quaint and naïve". In his study on unconscious motivations for practising psychotherapy, Sussman writes,

> [T]he clinical and conceptual simplicity of the one-person model of psychotherapy has long since vanished . . . [Those of us who practice psychotherapy can no longer afford not to explore our own motivations to heal. *Our opening question to clients "What brings you here?" must be posed to ourselves as well.* [*ibid.*, my italics]

Content and layout of the book

The outcome of our own reflective writing is explored and presented with reference to a survey targeting 280 other psychotherapists, and to literature in the area of therapists' motivations for practising as therapists.

Chapter One revolves around some of the basic beliefs by which we generate further knowledge about therapists and their motivations. This chapter touches on the subject of storytelling and considers the issue of how we may construe and understand ourselves as therapists.

Chapter Two explores the question of therapists' choice of career in a more general context, with reference to different theories and outlooks on the matter. What is "helping", and why do some people make it into their profession? What sort of images do we find in literature and research? Your own contribution is greatly encouraged; we are hoping that you will approach this book as the beginning of your own creation. This particular chapter revolves around what "other therapists" think. Two hundred and eighty counsellors and psychotherapists are approached, via already existing professional networks, with the question about why they chose to be a therapist. Two hundred and thirty-eight therapists replied, and their answers are presented in this chapter.

In Chapter Three, the replies from the survey will be considered in the context of reflective practice. Statistics offer an accessible overview to therapists' motivations for practice, but does not capture the ambiguity and complexity of meaning making. The survey highlights that two-thirds of the therapists refer to their own problems as a background to their present profession. However, the two most frequent categories, "childhood" and "adult life crisis", seem, perhaps not surprisingly, to mean different things for different people. This chapter revolves around the reflective learning approach to practice. Key terms, such as reflection-in-action and double-loop learning are introduced, together with more recent thinking within reflective practice in terms of reflexivity and critical reflection.

Chapters Four–Nine involve the outcome of our own reflective writing group. We are six different counsellors and psychotherapists, who reflect on the theme of why we have become therapists. Each of us represents the "categories" raised in the survey, albeit in our very different ways.

Chapter Ten revolves around the question "what have we learnt?", or what have we "found" with regard to the question of why therapists choose to be therapists.

Chapters One–Four and Chapter Ten are authored by me, Sofie Bager-Charleson. All chapters have, however, been subject to collaborative reading and response.

CHAPTER ONE

The way we "story" our experiences

*R*eflective writing is a term used for writing for the purpose of "making sense of ourselves and the world" (Bolton, 2005, p. 4). Rather than *storing* experiences like computers, we "story" them, asserts Bolton. Bolton, Field, and Thomson (2006, p. 2) contend that, "Writing is different from talking; it has a power all of its own . . . It can allow an exploration of cognitive, emotional and spiritual areas otherwise not accessible".

Reflective writing involves "examining our story making processes critically, to create and recreate fresh accounts of our lives from different perspectives, different points of view and to elicit and listen to the responses of peers" (Bolton, 2005, p. 3). To question our "story making" involves "deconstructing" (Pease & Fook, 1999) and examining the narratives that we hold about ourselves and our world, in this case about ourselves as professional helper. In Chapter Two, helping is referred to as being anything from "sparkling" moments to "psychological cannibalism".

Polkinghorne (1988, p. 14) refers to the significance of narratives on both a personal and a cultural level:

> Narratives perform significant functions. At the individual level, people have a narrative of their own lives, which enables them to

1

construe what they are and where they are headed. At the cultural level, narratives serve to give cohesion to shared beliefs and to transmit values.

Reflective writing

Reflective writing should not be confused with "purging", off-loading, or be seen as an outpouring in its own right. We have assumed that this would be of little interest to the reader.

As Smith (1985) describes, reflective writing usually involves at least three stages; pre-writing, writing, and rewriting. The pre-writing is often a scribbling and unstructured phase, perhaps not too different from "purging", if that is what is needed by the writer at the time. The actual writing involves organizing the unstructured thoughts into a more reader-friendly format: that is, with a reader in mind. The final stage is, perhaps, what earns this kind of writing its name: "reflective" writing (Bolton, 2005; Carter & Gradin, 2001; Smith, 1985; Winter, Buck, & Sobieschowska, 1999). This is a phase that entails exploring patterns and reoccurring themes in one's own way of organizing events. We do not, as Smith suggests, gain information about the world through direct contact.

> To perceive the world in the way it does, the brain must construct a theory of what the world is like. To do this, the brain must be creative . . . We work on our theory constantly, adding a touch here, modifying a part there, testing it continually against "experience" . . . [Smith, 1985, p. 33]

Talking and thinking involves fleeting processes; it is difficult to linger, return, and consider the different stages at which we make sense of our situations. Writing, on the other hand, offers what Smith refers to as "relative permanence". The words stay, to speak, accessible for us on the paper. The final stage, the rewriting stage, involves rereading your texts with themes and patterns, perhaps with blind spots or biases in mind.

Critical friend

An important part of this exercise is to write with a dialogue with someone else in mind; if you agree to write yourself in connection with this reading, you may write with a peer or with your supervisor either in mind or as an actual companion. During the writing of our respective "stories" for the second section of this book, writing with each other in mind was an important aspect. The term "critical friend" is often used in reflective practice. It has very little, if anything at all, to do with criticism. The point is usually rather to listen and feed back what you hear. Knott and Scragg (2008) refer to it as "mirroring". We tell each other what we see.

Our writing has involved reading each other's texts with the view of feeding back what we have "heard". Our response to each other's texts has revolved around questions such as; "I get the impression that your theme in this text is 'this' and that the essence of your experience is 'that'; have I got that right? Does that fit in with what you wanted the reader to hear?"

Beverley Taylor defines critical friends in this way,

> A *critical friend* can offer external perspective to extend your reflective capacity. "critical" in this sense does not mean criticizing, but being prepared to ask important questions and make tentative suggestions to unseat previous perception, to find other possibilities and insights. *A critical friend is chosen by you as some one you trust and respect.* [2006, p. 64, my italics]

We began our writing in a playful, relaxed way. Our first lines were part of a piece of uninterrupted writing; a writing without time to stop and think. We invite you to try for yourself.

The exercise below encourages further thinking about yourself as a "learner". For us, this was an important theme; all sorts of old prejudices surfaced once we knew we were going to "produce" something rather than holding, containing, and supporting others. We invite you to try this as your first exercise in reflective writing.

Your reflection

Uninterrupted writing

- Write for ten minutes without stopping. As Winter, Buck, and Sobieschowska (1999, p. 11) advise,

  Uninterrupted writing [means] to get down and write. If you can not think of the next word, then repeat the one you are writing until the one you need occurs to you. Don't spend time wondering what to write next.

- Allow yourself to travel back in time, to your childhood or adolescence. Continue writing without stopping to think from the sentence below;

  "It was a Wednesday morning, I scanned the room for my school shirt and I thought . . ."
- Stop after ten minutes
- Read your text. How did you find the writing?
- Compare yourself as a "learner" then and now. Is there anything which you bring with your from previous experiences into this context—for instance, with regard to writing?

Confidentiality

With its focus on themes and reoccurring patterns, our own reflective writing does not always follow exact events. In fact, we have encouraged each other to sieve out generic traits rather than listing separate events as they may have occurred in real life. In our case studies here, the clients are usually an amalgam of voices reflecting true events, albeit not in the order and way that they are referred to in our stories. A certain degree of artistic licence has not only been tolerated, but encouraged. We do not, for instance, expect you as a reader to be interested in our exact experiences in a *"then he came and I did that and she said"* way. We do not think that you would be interested in a long list of precise events. This is not what reflective writing is about.

We assume that what may be of value in the context of reflective writing are generic, abstracted themes sieved out of accumulated experiences. We have focused on experiences which we believe can be of a more general, possibly shared importance in the context of working as a therapist.

As Bolton (2005) points out, "reflective writing is not about confession". Confession implies that we disown our responsibility, or hand it over to someone else. Reflective writing is quite the opposite, as suggested earlier: a means to an end where we face, challenge, and sometimes reassess our ways of being.

The process is similar to that which we witness our clients do, as they explore their own trains of thought. Underlying values, beliefs, and constructs previously held as "facts" are explored and challenged. Familiar strategies are reassessed in light of an awareness that alternative framings of events are at hand. With this in mind, "narrative truth" proceeds "factual", or, as Polkinghorne (1988) puts it, "paradigmatic" truth. It is the meaning that the event is given that is being brought to the forefront, rather than the actual event itself.

So, none of us reveals exact client details; all of us have gone to considerable lengths in protecting our clients' anonymity, and, in doing so, artistic licence has played an important role.

Reflexive awareness

Reflexivity captures a prevalent theme in social and human sciences today, where the enquirer is encouraged to "own" her involvement, no matter what she investigates or engages with professionally. Finlay and Gough (2003, p. 5) write,

> Reflexivity in all its guises is now, arguably a defining feature of qualitative research . . . We realise that meanings are negotiated within particular contexts. [R]esearchers no longer question the need for reflexivity; the question of "how to do it?"

Counsellors and psychotherapists are just as likely as researchers to affect the outcome of the work due to their own personal investment. They are, as Finlay and Gough put it, "actively constructing the collection, selection and interpretation of data". Rosen and Kuehlwein (1996) conclude that this kind of outlook on practice ultimately rests on "constructivist beliefs" about "reality". They write, "There are a variety of constructivist models, they all hold in common the epistemological belief that a totally objective reality, one that stands apart from the knowing subject, can never fully be known" (p. 5).

Counsellors and psychotherapist with a constructivist outlook integrate their practice, as Weaver (2008, p. 2) puts it, "from the principle that there is more than one true judgement of the world. There is no absolute authority to whom we can turn to that will provide 'The Answer'".

In the second section of this book, we will all approach constructivism from different angles. In Sheila's story, a development within constructivism called social constructionism is highlighted. Informed by systemic theory, Sheila explores both her own childhood and her practice with reference to "social realities". Both constructivism and constructionism assume that meanings are created, rather than pre-existing and discovered, as implied earlier with reference to Smith (1985). Social constructionism focuses on relationships. As Gergen (2009, p. 3) puts it, "nothing is real unless people agree that it is . . . we may say that as we communicate with each other we construct the world in which we live". Constructivism places a greater importance on the individual than constructionism. Gergen (1996, in Rosen & Kuehlwein, pp. 15, 19) disaffiliates himself from the "Western individualism of constructivism". Social constructionism

> place[s] no emphasis upon intention, thought, feelings, or wishes of the individual human mind in isolation. It is on the everyday playing field of social exchange and in the relationships between individuals that understanding, knowledge, and meaning are created. [*ibid.*, p. 17]

This critique of "Western individualism" is pursued from different angles by other members of our group. Sherna reconstructs our concept of "self" with reference to intercultural theory on "several selves", and Susan's experience of "self" is approached in a transpersonal context, focusing on "the beyond" individuals and their human relationships. For those with a particular interest in social constructionism, Sheila's chapter will do the theory justice, and further reading is recommended, for instance, Gergen (1999). My own psychoanalytically-inspired thinking and Francesca's existential emphasis on the individual's authenticity and *dasein* bring further angles to our interpretation of reality. In this book, an overriding and shared perspective on our professional "judgements" is that they are personal, individual, subjective, *and* socio-culturally created interpretations in the sense that reflexivity implies.

Reflexivity embraces both personal and social influences. Counsellors and psychotherapists seem particularly well equipped to consider underlying meanings in the way we construct the world. "Objectivity is pretence", asserts Parker (1994); "even distance is a stance". The researcher is no longer regarded as a detached scientist; "the researcher is a central figure who actively constructs the collection, selection and interpretation of data" subjectivity in research is transformed from a problem to an opportunity', write Finlay and Gough (2003, p. 5). This thinking seeps into all areas of social and human studies, therapeutic practice included.

Construing ourselves as therapists

It will become obvious that some of our own stories relate to the categories referred to by the therapists in the survey. One therapist from the survey replied, for instance, that she embarked on her therapy career regarding herself as someone with an exceptional interest in people, only later recognizing how this extreme intuitive "talent for listening" rested on vigilance and fear. She had to become good at sensing moods and predicting changes in her parents, as she grew up with an alcoholic mother. The reply in the survey about vigilance resonated with me. My story will revolve around the dilemma involved in becoming a therapist on the basis of a set of motives that become reconstrued during training and my own personal therapy.

Inspired by psychoanalytical thinking, I focus on my choice to become a therapist with reference to unconscious motifs, in particular. I refer to a scenario that captures how I needed to re-think my career as a couple counsellor, and to discontinue it for a while. I refer to Andy and Jane, with the aim of illustrating how, as Sedgwick (2005, p. 110) puts it, the client's projections need a hook in the therapist to catch on to. "The carrier of projections is not just any object", wrote Jung, "but someone who offer a 'hook' to hang on".

"Unconscious" motivations are approached from different angles in this book. "Not taking things at face value" involves "exploring unconscious motivations", contends Sussman (1992), when raising questions around the therapists' motivations for their career. The concept "unconscious" is used in this book in a broad sense, ultimately in the sense that the reflective practice approach implies inviting the practitioner to "explore what is beyond the immediate line of vision" (Taylor, 2006). We do not approach the unconscious as a "thing" within a medical model, or as a great mystery, but more as "a reservoir of latent meaning" as Bateman and Holmes (1999, p. 9) put it. They approach the unconscious as a metaphor for affective meanings that we are unaware of until they emerge in, for instance, the therapeutic dialogue and relationship:

> With the shift in contemporary psychoanalysis away from mechanism toward meaning, "the unconscious" becomes a metaphor for the affective meanings of which the [person] is unaware of, and which emerges through the relationship with the analyst. "Unconscious" becomes an adjective rather than a noun: "unconscious processes", rather than "the unconscious". This links psychoanalysis with the "post-modern" notion of polysemy or multiple meanings which are to be found in any cultural phenomenon or "text". [*ibid.*]

The psychoanalytic perspective addresses transference and countertransference as means for new meanings to emerge. Another angle, which is a different way of framing the process where meanings and realities emerge through interactions, is explored by Sheila Lauchlan in her story about her practice, which is influenced by social constructionism. Sheila quotes Gergen, the father of social constructionism, who writes about "when our eyes are opened to seeing our blindness" through "collaborative discourse":

> [P]sychotherapy may be thought of as a process . . . the forging of meaning in the context of collaborative discourse. It is a process during which the meaning of experience is transformed via a fusion of the horizons of the participants, alternative ways of punctuating experience are developed, and a new stance toward experience evolves. [McNamee & Gergen, 1992, p. 8]

Sheila's story approaches childhood trauma through her systemic perspective and social constructionist thinking on the way our lives take shape. Sheila shares her experience of an early bereavement within her own family. In Sheila's case, ways of dealing with bereavement typical for the time and place where she grew up awakened a particular interest in socially held values and beliefs and how they affect the individual and her sense of self. Sheila works with families and couples in private practice.

As suggested, as the stories by the members of our reflective writing group evolve, categories referred to in the survey, such as "interest in people", "crisis in adulthood", and "childhood" become increasingly ambiguous. They mean different things to different people. We make different use of our experiences. The question "why do therapists choose to be therapists?" is a question with several layers. Another difference that emerges in our reflective writing is that we are all drawn to, and interested in, different aspects of therapy.

Francesca Thorpe explores her childhood experience in growing up with thalidomide. Francesca's reflections revolve around both socially held values and beliefs and the individual's sense of self. Francesca shares her experiences from a particular client encounter, where the issue of our sense of identity is considered with reference to both raw and painful emotions and, eventually, also made sense of in light of existential thinking about our being-in-the-world. Francesca muses over both how and why she practises as a therapist with reference to the existential proposition about freedom and responsibility for how we define ourselves in relation to others. We can strive, writes Francesca, for authentic living where we live according to "the values one recognizes as worth committing oneself". Francesca is interested, in other words, in dealing with the "givens", the unavoidable, in life. With her example from her work with Janet, Francesca reflects over how she deals with problems when the boundary between her own and the client's problems becomes blurred. Francesca works in schools, private practice, and is counselling within an international therapy project for victims of Thalidomide.

In the subsequent chapter, Sherna Ghyara Chatterjee shares the experiences that she feels have directed her career into therapy. Her particular focus revolves around how the individual develops a sense of self within a social context. Sherna grew up in India, and she brings us along on a journey leading up to her professional identity and sense of self today. She expands on the theme of intercultural therapy and shares her experiences of integrating a Freudian psychoanalytic thinking with an Indian understanding of self and reality. She reflects over influences on many different levels, in light of family customs and stories handed down through generations, but also with reference to historical and political developments. Do we need a "core identity"? asks Sherna. When considering herself in both personal and professional contexts, Sherna ponders on the theme that "All of us have an inner world which consists of internalized objects, which are from the external world. How much choice do we exercise in this?"

Sherna lives in India and the UK and works in private practice and within the National Health Service (NHS) as a psychoanalytic therapist informed by intercultural theory.

Susan McGrath shares her experiences of therapeutic practice with reference to a session where Susan's thinking about what brought her into therapy comes to the surface. While many of the other group members trace their motives for working as a therapist to childhood, in one way or another, Susan relates to the category of therapists who, in the survey, referred to "adult crisis" as a trigger for their interest in therapy. Susan explores her personal and professional experiences from a transpersonal perspective, focusing on the beyond. Susan is informed by synthesis, and works as a student counsellor and in private practice. She refers to the term "bi-focal vision" to describe her outlook on both life and therapeutic practice. Susan writes,

> Psychosynthesis hypothesizes that we have an "I", which is our divine essence beyond, but also includes our conditioning and wounding ... I am struck with the idea that therapy is not just about reducing anxiety or psychological symptoms, but about fulfilling potential and helping us to engage fully with all life has to offer from an authentic place.

Through her example with Amy, Susan brings the idea of a bi-focal vision alive, and she reflects on both how she responds to her clients and why she has chosen to work in the way that she does.

Pamela Critchley has chosen to share her interest and research in the area of self-disclosure. What are the ethical concerns in allowing our "selves" to come across in the room? Can we avoid it? Pam mixes research with her own musing and experience from the theme of when and how the therapist relates as a human being in the room, rather than as a mere "expert". Pam works in private practice with individuals and couples, informed by psychoanalytic, existential, and postmodern thinking.

In the final chapter, we explore the outcome based on the survey, and the literature, in combination with our own reflective writing. What is the outcome? What can we say about why therapists choose to be therapists?

CHAPTER TWO

Why do therapists choose to be therapists?

I n this chapter, therapists' motivation for practising as therapists will be explored with reference to books and research in the area. In addition, we will refer to a survey addressed to 280 counsellors and psychotherapists. You are also invited to consider your own motives.

A shameful question?

What prompts some people to make it into their profession to try to "help" people in emotional difficulty? What is it, to quote Guggenbuhl-Craig (2009, p. 3), "that compels people to want to help the sick, the suffering, the unhappy, the outcast?"

There are many books about "how" to practise as a therapist, but surprisingly few that raise the question of "why". This is odd, as Sussman (1992, p. 7) points out, given that psychotherapy "has had a good deal to say about the unconscious factors in the choice of occupation".

Sedgwick (2005, p. 1) concludes that "exposing" the therapists may "indeed collide with narcissistic–exhibitionistic issues". In fact, he compares the subject of the therapist's reactions to their clients with a "gynaecologist revealing fantasies about patients":

> This kind of writing [about the therapist's emotions] . . . is not intended for patients, though conceivably it could be informative for them too. It could be disturbing as well. As one female colleague noted, *this kind of writing is somewhat like a gynaecologist revealing fantasies about patients.* [*ibid.*, my italics]

It is, nevertheless a "subject that needs airing", writes Sedgwick. He is supported by therapists such as Kottler, Strupp, Guggenbuhl-Craig, Sussman, and Miller. Sedgwick continues,

> Are these things better left unsaid (or at least unwritten)? Perhaps so, as far as the patient is concerned. *On the other hand, the subject needs airing because it is real and it is denied, and it is an important topic for professionals.* [*ibid.*, my italics]

Sussman addresses the "hidden dangers" for therapists, as well as clients, when their motives remain unexplored. The rate of burnout is, for instance, high among therapists. Sussman cites Guy (1987, in Sussman, 1992, p. 244), who surveyed therapists' burnout symptoms. He found affective symptoms that included "anxiety, depression and despondency, loneliness, fearfulness, emotional exhaustion, helplessness, anger and irritability, feelings of guilt and self-doubt".

Sussman (1992, p. 245) also cites Kelly (1978) and Prochaska and Norcross (1983), who report a significant degree of career dissatisfaction among psychotherapists. Sussman (*ibid.*) writes,

> [A]fter twenty five years in the field, 46 percent of those surveyed expressed dissatisfaction with their careers in psychotherapy by indicating that they would not enter the field if they were to live their lives over again.

Even more alarmingly, research indicates "that therapists commit suicide at a rate that exceeds that of the general population" (Guy, 1985, cited in Sussman, 1992, p. 21) writes, "The most startling figure is that reported by Moore (1982). In her sample, female psychiatrists committed suicide at a rate forty-seven times that of the general population".

Kottler (1993, p. 176) supports the statistics about therapists struggling in silence. He asserts that "approximately 10 percent of practicing therapists are clinically depressed. Another 10 percent have problems with substance abuse. A significant number struggles with chronic illness (10 percent) and loneliness (8 percent)". Kottler 1993, p. 178) concludes, "It is unfortunate that when burnout does lead to significant impairment, it is the nature of the therapist's dysfunction to deny that there is anything wrong".

Helping and its sparkling moments

Should we need to ask the question? Is it not obvious that "helping" others is a beautiful thing; a meaningful action with its own, priceless reward? Rogers (1995, p. 19) refers to hearing someone "deeply" and unselfishly as a "sparkling moment" which puts him in contact with something "universal". He continues,

> When I am able to let myself be congruent and genuine, I often help the other person. When the other person is transparently real and congruent, he often helps me. In those rare moments when a deep realness in one meets a realness in the other, a memorable "I–Thou relationship" as Martin Buber would call it, occurs. Such a deep and mutual personal encounter does not happen often, but I am convinced that unless it happens occasionally, we are not living as human beings.

Rogers (*ibid.*, p. 8) uses the term deep hearing for "phenomenologically shared" (Yalom, 1980) moments; when otherwise separate experiences and perspectives are shared. The prospect of entering someone's experiential world is, by definition, an act of "surrendering" momentarily to what Buber (1946 [1971], p. 246) refers to as a "realm of between": "(W)here I and Thou meet, there is a realm of "between".

The philosopher Merleau-Ponty (1999, p. 200) describes this kind of meeting as a form of "merging": "Our perspectives merge into each other, and we exist through a common world".

Bion (1962) refers to "reverie". The child psychiatrist Daniel Stern (2004, p. 169) explores the idea of staying with "the other's phenomenology" or "entering [the other's] experiential world"

(Yalom, 1980, p. 17) through "now moments" or "kairos"-moments, which capture qualitative, "immeasurable" moments as opposed to quantitative shifts in therapy. Broden (2005) refers to them as "dyadic expansions of consciousness that can be achieved between patient and therapist in creating a system for mutual regulation of affect". From researching infants' and young children's interaction with their care-givers, Stern has observed the healing impact of brief moments when "each person intuitively partakes in the experience of the other". This temporary, "jointly lived" experience requires that the therapist abandon her "technically accepted response". Her presence is, however, essential; the meeting demands the therapist's "signature". Stern continues, "The nature of a now moment usually demands something beyond a technically acceptable response: It demands a moment of meeting . . . It must be spontaneous and must carry the therapist's personal signature, so to speak".

Contrary to Winnicott, Bowlby, and other leading object relations and attachment theory therapists, Stern's research coincides in time with "trailblazing" (Ghaemi, 2007) neuroscientific findings. This research makes previously tacit knowledge explicit, regarding what effect these encounters of mother–infant can have on the brain. It responds to the most basic need for human development. Connections and the growth within the orbital frontal cortex and other parts of the brain are affected by interaction and social stimulation. Schore (2008, p. 23) uses the concept "neuropsychoanalysis" to describe these "recent [integrative] models that view . . . influences from the social environment as imprinted into the biological structures".

Neurobiological research could also be argued to illustrate what existentialists have proposed for decades with regard to the phenomenologically shared moment. The reciprocal nature of these encounters implies that, as Rogers proposed, without these "deep and mutual personal encounters . . . we are not living as human beings"—perhaps neither therapist nor client.

The shadows

There are, of course, many different ways of looking at counselling and psychotherapy. We will have the opportunity to approach talking therapies from several angles in this book. Your own involvement will be particularly welcome.

One relatively undisputed opinion seems to be that the road to an accredited status for a therapist is "long and arduous", as Sussman (1992, p. 3) puts it. In his book about unconscious motivations for practising psychotherapy, Sussman addresses a less "sparkling" side of talking therapies:

> Having arrived, the practitioner of psychotherapy is often emotionally taxed; the process is frequently characterized by a good deal of anxiety, ambiguity and doubt. The therapeutic outcome, moreover, is always uncertain. *Given this forbidding scenario*, it seems remarkable that anyone enters what Freud (1973) deemed one of "those impossible professions in which one can be sure beforehand of achieving unsatisfying results. *What are the underlying motivations that provide the impetus for such an undertaking?*" [my italics]

Each year, hundreds of counsellors and psychotherapists apply for accredited status from their member organizations, such as the BACP or the UKCP. During 2009 alone, the BACP accepted 1012 new members, and the UKCP registered 476 new members. It is impossible to count all the institutes, colleges, and universities that provide training for a career as a counsellor or psychotherapist. In monthly magazines for BACP and UKCP members, the number of courses advertised in January 2010 exceeded the number of vacant positions.

Most trainings options require up to four years' training, sometimes more. During this period, the trainee is required to undertake his or her own personal therapy and volunteer at a placement for several hours. Six hundred and fifty training and 650 unpaid practice hours, as in my own case, is not an unusual requirement. At the end of each training, we can rest assured that the supply of counsellors and psychotherapists invariably will exceed the demand.

This cumbersome training is usually generally accepted as important from a self-reflective stance. Skovholt and Ronnestad (1995, 2003) identify phases and themes in counselling training. They conclude that "An active, exploratory, searching, and open attitude is of extreme importance. Asking for and receiving feedback is crucial" (Skovholt & Ronnestad, 1995, p. 107).

There is, however, a risk that therapists are assumed to be "repaired", fixed, and once and for all "relieved from all evil" after such a challenging training. As Sussman (1992, p. 246) addresses, "unlike traditional shamans, modern day healers are expected to be psychologically strong, robust and stoical". This is an assumption that can backfire. Sussman continues,

> [T]hose who become openly depressed or anxious are liable to be viewed by colleagues as somehow inferior or weak . . . As incongruous as it may seem, the professional that aims to assist people in accepting and coming to terms with their feelings and needs often fails to tolerate or to even acknowledge such human concerns in its practitioners. [*ibid.*]

Not so sparkling

Alice Miller is suspicious of the unique sensitivity required to create the previously mentioned "sparkling" moments of deep encounter. Miller (1997, pp. 20, 60) questions the therapist's willingness to surrender herself to the world of others, no matter how "shared" it might feel. "The therapist's acute sensibility, empathy, responsiveness and powerful 'antennae' indicates that as a child he probably used to fulfil other people's need and to repress his own".

Miller warns of a need to recreate situations where we seek our lost "love" from our parents, whom we were once compelled to gratify at the cost of our own emotional development:

> I think that our childhood fate can indeed enable us to practice psychotherapy, but only if we have been given the chance, through our own therapy, to give up the most fragrant of our illusions. This means *tolerating the knowledge that, to avoid losing the 'love' of our parents, we were compelled to gratify their unconscious needs at the cost of our own emotional development*. . . . [The therapist] will discover in himself a need to live according to his true self and no longer forced to earn "love" that always left him empty-handed, since it is given to his false self. [my italics]

The Jungian analyst, Guggenbuhl-Craig, also expresses concern about "helpers" who try to "escape their own shadow" through their clients. He writes,

The profession of psychotherapy has many features in common with the other "helping professions" . . . Part of the training of social workers, nurses, teachers, doctors etc, should emphasize that the problem of the case or the patient are one's own as well . . . *it would be a great improvement to meet fewer of them who see illness only in their patients.* [1991, pp. 108, 125, my italics]

Sedgwick emphasizes the "ability to be wounded", and writes about the Jungian reference to Asklepios; "the wounded physician",

By heavily accenting the analyst's vulnerability . . . Jung depend the countertransference issue. It is no longer the analyst's openness, "mental health" or "knowledge" that is the major determinant; rather it is his own hurt that gives him the measure of his power to health (Jung, 1951, p. 116). Jung invokes the myth of Asklepios, the "wounded physician". There is the idea here of a healer with an incurable wound, and *paradoxically it is that very woundedness that mediates the healing power.* [2005, p. 15]

Strean (1998a, p. 14) agrees on the value of being "wounded".

When an analyst can truly see in himself conflicts similar to the ones the patient currently expresses, and when he faces the fact that patient and therapist are similar, this is when he hits therapeutic awareness.

Strean contends that each therapist has their "wounded speciality". He writes,

My father was too afraid of his anger to confront those who frustrated him. He preferred instead to pack up all his possessions and move . . . Through my experience of warding of feelings of helplessness and weakness, desperation, and anger when a patient threatens to leave, I have become an expert in dealing with such patients . . . I am particularly sensitive to those conflicts that provoke patients to want to leave treatment. [1998b, p. 127]

Chernin (1986, 1991) refers to her experience of being a daughter and a woman as invaluable experience for working with girls suffering from eating disorders. She often uses her "wounds" from her own eating disorder and relationship with her mother, a house-wife whom Chernin "surpassed" (1986, p. 22), lacking other devel-opmental models than "the ancient myth of Laius and Oedipus meeting for [whom the girls] bloody confrontation will not serve".

Symington quotes Klauber (1976, cited in Symington, 1986, p. 329) who contends that "patient and analyst need one another";

> But the analyst also needs the patient in order to crystallize and communicate his own thoughts, including some of his inmost thoughts on intimate human problems which can only grow organ-ically in the context of his relationship. They cannot be shared and experienced in the same immediate way with a colleague, or even with a husband or wife.

Sussman (1992, p. 235) emphasizes the tentative nature of his conclusion to his own research into "unconscious motivations for practicing psychotherapy", due to its "small sample group and methodological weakness". Nevertheless, he addresses support for his "hypothesis that an important determinant of the desire to prac-tice psychotherapy involves the attempt to come to terms with one's own psychological conflicts".

Through fourteen interviews with voluntary participants, Suss-man distilled a wide range of disturbances among the practising therapists. In practically all cases, he found signs of either past or ongoing disturbances. The extracts below offer an overview of some of the most frequent issues, together with randomly chosen extracts from the interviews. Sussman (1992, p. 180) observed, for instance, the following.

- Problems with family members

  "I think my mother was full of loss and self-absorbed"

- Voyerism

  "I thought that might be a very interesting part of the work, a sort of private, secret chamber of therapist and patient that really wasn't so different from sharing your secrets with a priest"

- Exhibitionism

  "I think that I have lots of actress in me that's frustrated at this point"

- Masochistic tendencies

  "[I am being] used as an instrument who is smashed against the wall, thrown out of the window, kicked . . . [laughs] made to feel enormously sad. Just the enormous range of emotions I get subjected to on a daily basis in my body, mind, soul and the accumulative effect over the years of being a container for all that intense emotion"

- Narcissistic needs

  "I was not allowed to be competent at home"

- Aggrandizes ego-ideal

  "[. . . not so different from being a priest] Within [our] Catholic church, to become a priest is the highest achievement. Priests are the most grand, powerful, important figures. They get to wear beautiful vestments, smell of incense and hear confessions, conduct masses and offer communion"

Page (1999, p. 2) agrees that each therapist comes with a dark side, and uses himself as an example:

[If] I am to apply the honest self-reflection I would hope to see in others, then I must accept that *somewhere in my psyche lurks the belief that I am beyond . . . mundane* matters . . . If left unchecked it might develop into an absurd . . . belief that I am omnipotent, beyond human vulnerability. [my italics]

Fromm (1998, p. 259) writes about therapists' inhibitions and boring lives, "*Many analysts become analysts because they feel inhibited* to reach human beings, to relate to human beings, and *in the role of an analyst they feel protected*" [my italics].

Reik (1948, in Sussman, 1992, p. 149) goes as far as to suggest that "the psychological comprehension of another person involves a sublimated form of [a] wish for incorporation, representation in a sense, "*psychological cannibalism*" [my italics].

Wosket (2003, p. 194) reacts against the tendency to procrastinate in all "helpers". It distracts from the fact that we actually often do help: "[T]he dire warning in much of the literature about the dangers of therapists' arrogance and narcissism . . . can [cause us] to shy away from claiming that we ever help".

However, Wosket (*ibid.*) agrees that the strong feelings in the counselling relationship often is a "taboo area" when it comes to the counsellor's own feelings. It is particularly difficult, writes Wosket, "to give ourselves permission to bring our sexual selves into our counselling relationship". Wosket refers to an American study (Pope et al., 1986), which revealed that "95% of men and 76% of women therapists had felt sexually attracted to clients on at least one occasion . . . 9.4% of men and 2.5% of women had acted on these feelings".

Storr (1979) concludes that the requirements on the psychotherapists are both unusual and challenging;

> The therapist's task is difficult. He has to be affected without acting upon his own feelings: *to feel, but to use his own feeling in the service of the patient . . . This requires considerable control and self-abnegation* . . . The capacity for self-abnegation is, I think unusual . . . It is certainly one of the more peculiar features of the practice of psychotherapy that the therapist spends the bulk of his professional life in situations in which his self expression is forbidden, or at least severely restricted . . . *His own personality is never fully expressed, but always orientated toward the need of the other . . . Successful therapists, I think, generally possess an especial capacity for identifying with the insulted and injured.* [pp. 172–173, my italics]

Viscott (1998) and Weinberg (1998) support this thesis about self-abnegation. Weinberg (1998, p. 28) quotes the poet Tennyson, who wrote, "The therapist remains the one who roams with a hungry heart". Weinberg continues, "The desire to help others [is] often a way of belonging, of being sure that others will return to them".

What brings you here?

As Sussman (1992, p. 7) points out, "[Therapy] has had a good deal to say about the general question of the role of unconscious factors in the choice of occupation . . . Is the activity of the therapist or analyst the exception to the rule?"

Is it difficult and unusual for therapists to talk about their underlying motivations? What do you think? We would like to invite you to consider your own conscious and unconscious motivations.

Please allow some space to consider your own conscious and unconscious motivations for practising counselling or psychotherapy. Below are some prompts that may help you.

WHY I CHOOSE TO BE A THERAPIST

Which of the following resonates most with you?

1. I have always been *interested in people*.
2. I enjoy the analytical, investigative element of therapy most.
3. The *flexible working hours* were essential when considering a career.
4. I believe that my *own childhood* influenced my choice of career.
5. A *crisis in later life* brought me into therapy and raised my interest in working as therapist myself.
6. *Nothing* of the above resonates with me; *instead* I choose to work as a therapist because of . . .

Your reflection

- Which number(s) did you choose?
- Please write for ten minutes about anything that comes into your head when you think of the topic "why I choose to be a therapist".
- Read your text. What does it feel to write and read about yourself? Does your text reflect what you really think or feel?

The next section in this chapter revolves around the attempt to learn more about the motivations for a therapy career by asking others and by considering possible themes in the literature review.

Moving between a personal and a general level

An important part of this project has been to explore our own motives *in the context* of others. This had involved a balance between "owning" the question, on a personal level, and "disowning" it enough to bring it up on a level that involves others. Reflective writing has played an essential role in this process, where we, as individuals, have been able to generalize and compare our own experiences in a contained, safe environment. Another step involved exploring 280 other therapists and, as suggested, "reading up" on the matter.

Peer group dynamic and feedback in our reflective writing group

During the creation of our six "stories", many new feelings surfaced. The process involved both creativity and frustration. What struck us all in the beginning was how "self indulgent" it felt, not only to raise the question in the first place, but also with regard to writing texts for publishing purposes. Some of us recalled failures from school. Others, like myself, felt vulnerable without my "helper" role during my own writing. There was, as suggested earlier, a great deal of excitement, and some of us experienced new sides of ourselves both on a personal creative level and professionally with regard to our clients and what we wanted to invest our resources in.

Some of the members identified changes within the group. Envy and competition were some new feelings that crept in and needed to be highlighted and discussed. We began to explore our perceptions of ourselves and each other, both on a personal level and also with reference to social values and beliefs. It felt, for instance, alien and almost "masculine", as one of us put it, to want to write a book. Our roles as helpers and supporters seemed to be a multi-layered issue.

The wider therapeutic community

Another important aspect was to engage in a dialogue outside our reflective writing group. As mentioned, we knew each other well, and it felt both threatening and, in the long run, positive to secure feedback from "outsiders". We belonged to a larger peer group, the Surrey Counselling and Psychotherapy Initiative, with over fifty members. We made a point of discussing the project with our colleagues in this group. This resulted both in valuable feedback and in our writing group changing slightly: one valued member decided not to write at this point in her life, and two new members joined the group.

Questionnaire

Through work, personal contacts, and general networks, a wide selection of practitioners was reached within the therapeutic community. My role as academic adviser on a doctoral programme for psychotherapists facilitated further enquiries of a more systematic research nature; this is something that really interests me. The survey consisted of a questionnaire with six options for choosing to be a therapist. This was emailed through networks, targeting integrative and humanistic counsellors and psychotherapists in particular. The email survey reached 280 accredited counsellors and psychotherapists, and received 238 replies.

Initially, the therapists were invited to expand on the theme of why they chose to become a therapist "in their words". Only five out of 280 therapists replied. The next attempt involved a simpler design. Six motives were listed, whereby one was offered the option of listing a motive not yet mentioned. Each therapist was emailed the same six options as you were on p. 23 in this book. They were asked to choose one or more motives. Two hundred and thirty-eight counsellors and psychotherapists replied in total. Only thirty elaborated on their choice; the majority replied with one or more numbers.

Literature review

Another important aspect of comparing views and expanding our own horizons of understanding was through reading about what others have to say about therapists and their motivations. As suggested earlier, our literature review implies that some "good" therapists approach their work with an unselfish "merging" in mind. There is, suggests both humanistic and psychoanalytical research, an underlying relational need, which often comes across as altruistic and more "noble" than the image of the "wounded healer" does. Rogers (1962, p. 18) refers to helping in terms of "connecting about the commonality of being a human being". As mentioned, Rogers muses on motives as rewarding and unselfish: he writes, "I have found it highly rewarding when I can accept another person . . . I have found it enriching to open channels".

Miller (1997) and Guggenbuhl-Craig (2009) are, as already mentioned, suspicious of a one-dimensional positive view on the role of the helper. Sussman (1992, p. 242) writes about "dangers of deficient self-knowledge" when "helpers" only offer altruistic motives for their choice to make helping others their profession.

It is, nevertheless, a commonly held belief that professions such as therapy, nursing, teaching, etc., are professions chosen on the basis of the inherent interest in human beings, rather than, for instance, because of monetary rewards.

In the following section, reasons and motives will be explored further, with reference to a survey distributed via email to 280 counsellors and psychotherapists. Their replies are referred to in terms of diagrams and tables, with some additional comments volunteered by the therapists who elaborated on their chosen "numbers".

Survey results

As you can see from Figure 1, only 15% chose "interest in people" as their overriding motivation for choosing to be a therapist.

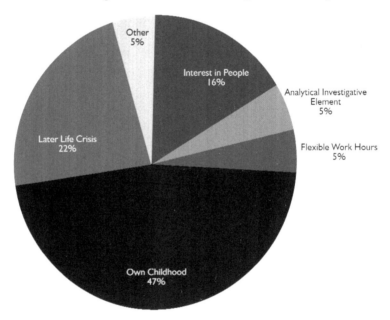

Figure 1.   The overall survey results in percentages.

Almost half of the therapists who replied to our survey implied that it was their "own childhood" which brought them into this career. Another 22% referred to a "later life" crisis.

As mentioned, only a few elaborated on their replies. With so few replies, it is difficult to know what "childhood" means. For those who did reply, it seemed to mean quite different things.

Childhood means different things

Some referred to an "unemotional unavailable environment".

"I grew up in an emotionally unavailable household, very cold."

"I was in and out of foster care as a child. I studied to be a social worker at first, but became interested in counselling. I work with drug counselling."

"I was adopted."

"I wanted to understand myself and my family."

"I'd say that I was such a good listener because of the fear that I had with me from an abusive childhood. It took me years to come to terms with that in my own personal therapy. Of course, I wouldn't trust my therapist to do me any good either at first. I had always had to look after myself. So, number 4 is my answer. I can honestly add number 1 now, but at the start it was a mess."

"We never ever spoke about feelings when I grew up. This left me feeling very inadequate for many years. I felt odd for having emotions . . ."

"I came from a very angry household. Dysfunctional, to say the least. I work with children in placement now, and my own experiences of a violent household are important. I can see when a child is frightened; they cover it up. That's usually the tragedy, frightened children are difficult to like. They push people away, when they need help the most."

Others referred to childhood in terms of positive role models.

"My particular interest was first sparked by my aunt, with whom I was always close; she is a clinical psychologist and was head of psychology at X University of X for years."

"I have always been interested in people and how they work: my parents worked in psychiatry and with social care."

"I was a frequent confidante to my friends when I was little and liked the idea of helping others. Then in training I became intrigued by what it means to be helpful and who is being helper."

Almost sixty therapists (Figure 2) referred to a crisis in adulthood.

"When I lost my job my world turned upside down."

"It was a crisis—the breakdown of my first marriage—that got me to therapy in the first place."

"I was fortunate enough to adopt ... [But] as each year passed things seemed to get worse and the strain of caring for one of the children was having a negative affect on the whole family. I was determined not to allow the placement to break down but the strain of holding things together had become overwhelming and I became stressed. This is when I sought counselling."

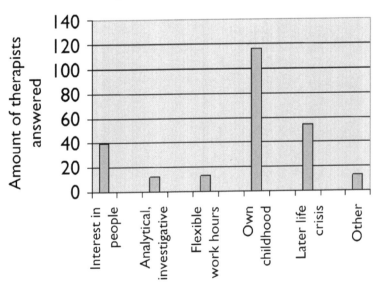

Figure 2. Replies divided among the 238 therapists.

Combined factors

Several therapists included either their own childhood and adult crises as one of two replies. Almost half of the population gave adult crisis as their second reply. Figure 3 indicates the distribution of first and second answers among the replies.

Some therapists elaborated on the combination of childhood and adult crises in terms of feeling poorly equipped to deal with an adult crisis.

"[We never ever spoke about feelings when I grew up. This left me feeling very inadequate for many years. I felt odd for having emotions] which of course made the death of my partner so extra difficult to deal with. I find again and again that clients bring these kind of problems, it is as if they think they are going mad for having strong feelings. My own experiences of that has made me extra sensitive to that, I think."

"[I came from a very angry household . . .] Without really knowing why at the time I decided never to have children myself. My partner at the time really wanted children, and it was this that brought us into couple therapy in the end. Our marriage ended in spite of

Figure 3.   Distribution of the replies.

it, and I see that as mainly my problem . . . To cut a long story short, I realized in therapy just how abusive my upbringing had been. I have been in therapy for six years, and I feel ready to move on. I'd like to give something back, and I feel that I can do that through my own work with kids now."

One therapist elaborates on the combination of (1) interest in people and (5) adult crisis.

"Mine is a mixture of 1 and 5. An initial general curiosity, about how people ticked and human behaviour. This was intensified when I found I was unable to have children."

A curiosity about how relationships and people "tick" was referred to by several therapists. One therapist writes about how her interest in relationships was nourished by witnessing her sisters becoming mothers.

"I became increasingly interested in my two sisters' different styles of parenting, their parent–child interactions and the children's behaviour. As an observer, supporter, and often agony aunt to my sisters, I felt a need to understand child behaviour and parent inter-action and wanted to know how things went wrong and what parents could do."

For some, more factors than two were included. The therapist below refers to a combination of an interest in people, own child-hood experiences, and an adult event/crisis.

"I have marked three (1, 4, 5) criteria . . . It was important in my family to have an 'interesting' career. Something that seemed worthwhile . . . I have always been interested in people and psychology . . . A careers assessment that I underwent at a time when I had dropped out and was entirely uninterested in any career suggested psychology and social work. It was a crisis—the breakdown of my first marriage—that got me to therapy in the first place. I found it exciting and fascinating; I've been passionate about therapy ever since.

Common features

We will probably never know to what extent the additional com-ments represent the total population of answers in terms of chosen numbers/categories of motives for becoming a counsellor or a psychotherapist. However, what does seem to stand out among those who did volunteer additional comments was how the term "crisis" was used in a positive sense. In most cases, "crisis" is referred to in terms of something of a eye opener;

"[When I lost my job my world turned upside down]. *I am glad now that it made me look at the world differently. I value other things now. My own personal therapy changed my outlook on life."*

"[It was a crisis - the breakdown of my first marriage] *that got me to therapy in the first place. I found it exciting and fascinating; I've been passionate about therapy ever since."*

"I would have answered (1) if you asked me at the beginning of my training! I see now that it was more about vigilance . . . in the beginning I just felt I was cut out for this kind of job. I would take in everything in the room and my supervisor would tell me that I was being so very emotionally sensitive and astute. *But really, I was frightened. My own therapy helped me to recognize that."*

"[The bereavement counselling opened my eyes for a completely different way of being.] *I was used to sales and that sort of thing. Counselling opened up a whole new world for me, very different from sales. But it was also through my own counselling that I realized what a secondary place emotions used to have in our household."*

"[I was fortunate enough to adopt . . . As each year passed things seemed to get worse and the strain of caring for one of the children was having a negative affect on the whole family. I was determined not to allow the placement to break down but the strain of holding things together had become overwhelming and I became stressed. This is when I sought counselling.] *I found it an immensely enlightening and enriching experience and from the very first session I wanted to be a counsellor too"*.

In conclusion

Not surprisingly, perhaps, there is a mixture of reasons in the therapists' accounts of why they chose to be therapists. It seems difficult, if not inappropriate, to position the replies in the context of the "camps" implied through the literature review. This, somehow, implies a split between the "good" and the "bad" therapists. It would feel alien to categorize the replies as reflecting *either* the image of (a) therapists who are motivated solely by what Rogers refers to as the "enriching understanding", where understanding others puts both client and therapist in touch with "communality", as Rogers puts it, in what "it means to be a human being", or (b) therapists who seek only to "repair" their own childhood through their clients, usually driven by dark ulterior motives.

What seemed to be a uniting theme in the replies was the "eye opening factor". Whether it related to a childhood event or an adult crisis, or simply a general interest in people, the personal experience of therapy had thrown light on prior experiences in ways that altered their career, family lives, and/or general outlook on life.

We cannot deny that an overwhelming 75% referred to personal experiences, largely dominated by some form of crisis. Returning to Sussman's book, which is likely still to be the most extensive survey about therapists' motivations, our results should come as no surprise. Storr proposes that the majority of psychotherapists choose to do so "for the wrong reasons";

> I once had a conversation with the director of a monastery. "Everyone who comes to us", he said, "does so for the wrong reasons." The same is generally true of people who become psychotherapists. It is sometimes possible to persuade people to become psychotherapists who have not chosen the profession for their own personal reason, but, for the best part, we have put up with what we can get, namely, ourselves. [1979, p. 165]

Storr, Sedgwick, and Sussman emphasize that this "pathology" is neither altogether good nor altogether bad. It is not so much a question about *what* has happened as of *how* the event and experience is being "known and utilized" (Sedgwick, 2005). Sussman concludes that the ability to identify with other people's emotional suffering is linked to the ability to reflect over and learn from one's own suffering:

> Not everyone who has suffered and can identify with emotional suffering in others will be an effective therapist. These characteristics must be coupled with the following features: the capacity to control such identifications; the experience of having learned from

one's own suffering, and thereby having matured; and the capacity for synthesizing pleasurable, as well as painful, life experiences. [1992, p. 249]

The idea of transforming experiences into something "useful" will be explored further in the following chapter. The question "why do you practise as a therapist?" will be explored from a slightly different angle; not only with regard to what has happened to the therapists, but how are his or her experiences transformed into the decision to be a therapist?

Your reflection

- Consider a problem from your own life, which you feel that you have been able to learn from and "make use of" in a constructive sense.

CHAPTER THREE

Reflective practice

This chapter revolves around reflective practice. The answer to *why therapists choose to be therapists* is only partly answered through statistics. Our inclination for moving "beyond face value", as addressed by Sussman, seems to be poorly matched by this statistic. It will not tell us much about the meaning-making processes which usually occupy our attention, as therapists.

Hearing reflexively

Reflexivity has already been introduced as something of increasing importance for practitioners and researchers dealing with social and human realities. This has certainly affected our own confidence in exploring the issue of therapists' own motivations in the first place. Sussman highlights how the focus on the relationship between practitioner and clients has changed;

> Therapists may be forgiven if at times they look back wistfully on the days when the clinical focus was squarely on the client, and the psychodynamics of the therapist were largely overlooked. The

clinical and conceptual simplicity of the one-person model of psychotherapy has long since vanished. [1992, p. 259]

As mentioned earlier, reflexivity (Alvesson & Skoldeberg, 2001; Banister, Burman, Parker, Taylor, & Tindall, 1994; Etherington, 2004; Finlay & Gough, 2003; Parker, 2004) is a frequently used term in research nowadays. It has developed in response to the assumption that social and human sciences deal with a "messy" reality. As suggested, reflexivity encourages us to "own" our involvement and to consider carefully what we "bring with us" into work, in terms of our personal past, cultural values, and belief. Fook (quoted in Stuart & Whitmore, p. 157, in White, Fook, & Gardner, 2008) writes,

> What we see and understand in a situation is influenced by our "subjectivity" including our embodiment (e.g., race, gender, social position, sexual orientation, ability, age) biography, values, ethics, emotions, cognitive and theoretical constructions.

This is the angle from which we approach the question of not only *how* to practise, but *why* we do so in the first place. How is the decision to practise influenced by our "subjectivity"?

Kondrat (quoted in Gardner, p. 145, in White, Fook, & Gardner, 2008) distinguishes between three "alternative perspectives on practice". These are reflective self-awareness, reflexive self-awareness and critical reflexivity.

Reflective self-awareness involves the capacity to be aware of our own biases and preferences, for instance, through the choice of theory and way of relating to our clients. What knowledge do we choose to bring with us into the room; what is our knowledge-in-use? Are we congruent with our "espoused theories"; the theories we claim to commit to? In the case studies, which are our own respective stories, each group member attempts to reflect on the choice of modality as part of considering the career choice as a whole. The discussions and the reading of each other's texts have prompted new ways of looking at our own prior understanding.

Reflexive self-awareness is usually a familiar concern for most therapists. Countertransference and congruence are examples of core concepts geared towards an understanding of what is going on for the therapist during their "hearing" of their clients. Again, each of us will approach this in different ways, depending on our psychoanalytic, existential, systemic, and transpersonal outlook.

Critical reflexivity is, in comparison, a relatively new concern, and involves questioning our relationship to our own culture. Critical reflexivity concerns the link between ourselves and our social structure. Gardner (in White, Fook, & Gardner, 2008) writes,

> Being "critical" adds an expectation of exploring practice in the context of the social system in which it operates, looking, for example, at the influence of social expectations about such issues as gender or age, class or ethnicity. [p. 145]

In our stories, cultural and social values are important considerations, we have each tried to reflect and discuss our sense of identity and our subsequent choice of profession in a cultural and social context. This is difficult, to a certain extent, impossible. Schön and Rein (1994) stress the importance of considering "metacultural frames", conditioned by the particular society and cultural understanding of our time. Bolton (quoted in Gardner, p. 145, in White, Fook, & Gardner, 2008) emphasize that "we all wear culturally tinted lenses through which we view the world". Hawkins and Shohet (2006) illustrate this dilemma with a Chinese proverb that says, "The last one to know about the water is the fish". Habermas (1987) says that it is like gravity; we do not realize how firmly we stand on the ground and how unshakable it usually is, until there is an earthquake. We are surrounded by our own culture, it is incorporated into our daily routines; we are influenced from all directions.

Double loop learning

Schön's idea of double loop learning is helpful when we try to conceptualize our underlying personal, cultural, and theoretical judgements and motivations for "entering the room".

Reflective practice involves, stresses Schön, a relationship based on a *reflective contract*, where the practitioner commits him or herself to a degree of openness and a genuine interest in how others perceive reality. Such practice rests on the understanding of "truth"(s) and "knowledge" as things that grow out of the client's interaction with her environment; knowledge is, in this sense, something that is socially constructed rather than already fixed givens or natural laws. Schön says (cited in Winter, Buck, & Sobieschowska, 1999, p. 184), "In the constructionist view, our perceptions, appreciations and beliefs are rooted in the worlds of our own making that we come to accept as reality".

Schön's theory on reflective practice explores two different ways of assessing our motivations on an everyday basis. He distinguishes (Argyris & Schön, 1978, pp. 2–3) between single loop and double loop learning;

> *Single-loop learning* is like a thermostat that learns when it is too hot or too cold and turns the heat on or off. The thermostat can perform this task because it can receive information (the temperature of the room) and take corrective action.

> *Double-loop learning* occurs when error is detected and corrected in ways that involve the modification of an organization's underlying norms, policies, and objectives.

We can, in this sense, choose to stay with immediately accessible information in the room. When something "goes wrong", we can explore other strategies and technical measures within already defined goal and values adhered to in our respective modalities. Hawkins and Shohet (2006) offer an example: "For instance a supervisee might learn within a single loop that clients may be erratic in their attendance if a clear contract is not made".

Single loop is "completed within a single coherent frame of references" (Hawkins & Shohet, 2006, p. 79). It concerns explicit, expressed, and often officially adhered to objectives and strategies. I have borrowed a model (Figure 4) from my earlier book about reflective practice (Bager-Charleson, 2010). Sometimes, it helps to visualize things. Figure 4 refers to a straightforward reasoning, with an eye on obvious cause and effects. This usually involves an "expert" stance to work. We assume that there is an "objective" cause-and-effect-related explanation. Rowan and Jacobs (2002) explore this kind of technical approach to work in terms of an "instrumental stance", with its explicit focus on "curing" with already set "facts" at hand. We will soon return to this.

An alternative response is to question the goals and values themselves, to subject them to critical scrutiny (Figure 5). In this

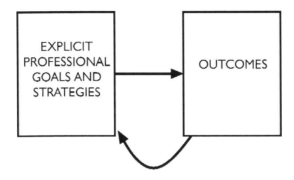

Figure 4.   Single loop learning with a cause and effect thinking.

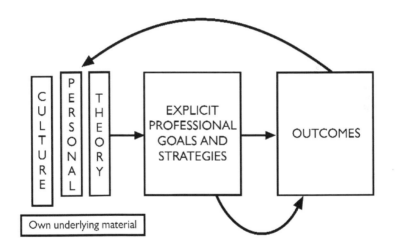

Figure 5.   Double loop learning challenges our own underlying cultural, personal, and theoretical values.

case, we question the strategies with regard to how they came about in the first place? What purpose do they serve? What underlying values and beliefs do they hold? To what extent does our own material come into the equation? Do we actually practise as we preach; maybe we have "distorted" the original strategy slightly, without thinking much about it?

With reference to the contract scenario above, Hawkins and Shohet continue,

> "[B]ut when the learning has a double loop they may understand, for example, why they are drawn not to make a clear contract with the client who shares with them the difficulty in accepting authority. [The second learning loop] explores attitude, values and assumptions. This second loop ensures that the learning is deepened beyond the most obvious. [2006, p. 78]

Double loop learning helps to expand our analytical frame "beyond the obvious" (Taylor, 2008) to explicitly identify and challenge underlying cultural, personal, and theoretical assumptions.

Double loop learning is actually quite obvious thinking for many therapists. The list is literally endless, with books exploring how our unaddressed underlying motivations can lead to a mismatch between strategies and outcomes for *clients*. Double loop learning is, in this sense, familiar territory to most counsellors and psychotherapists, but, as suggested, usually with the client in mind.

An essential aspect of double loop learning in this context is that (a) we are always learners; we develop our "maps" of reality constantly. It also assumes that (b) the therapist brings personal shadows and "culturally tinted" spectacles into the room.

Schön's theory on reflective practice draws on generic traits within what Guggenbuhl-Craig refers to as the "ministering professions". Reflective practice implies moving "beyond the obvious" on several levels. Schön encourages us to challenge the framework that we know, with an interest in avoiding "intractable controversies" between camps of professionals such as social workers, politicians, teachers, and psychotherapists. Schön draws our attention to the "comfort" that professionals normally draw from their professional frameworks. They give us a sense of belonging; we often identify ourselves with reference to an "us and them" thinking. Some would argue that practitioners are unable to move between frameworks without losing a sense of purpose and direction in the work. Schön and Rein (1994, p. xiii) write,

> For example, the contemporary sociologist, Joseph Gusfield, has written that "the clinician, the practitioner, the official, cannot afford to stand outside the framework within which action occurs,

to examine their institutions and beliefs as only one among a number of possible worlds". If practitioners were to do this. Gusfield believes, they would have to give up that wholehearted commitment to a single set of institutions and beliefs that is indispensable to their effective action.

Double-loop learning invites the practitioner to consider our frameworks in light of underlying assumption, with the hope of reaching *beyond* familiar goals and strategies. It encourages us to understand and confront our own framings with questions such as: *what underlying cultural, personal and/or theoretical beliefs and assumption do I bring with me into the room?*

Underlying personal material

Casement explores his own underlying personal motivations with reference to the question; "what am I putting into the analytic space?" He writes,

> [W]e are encouraged *not to allow ourselves to be led by any wish of our own* . . . It is an admirable aim, *often honoured more in principle than in practice.* [I]n order to help me monitor myself in each session, I have learned to think of the analytic space. *I am asking myself: "Who is putting what into this space?"* [2008a, p. 155, my italics]

Casement distinguishes between countertransference and what he calls "mirroring" to illustrate this kind of double loop thinking. In his book *Learning from Our Mistakes*, Casement (2008b) refers to "tricky" situations and "mis-communications" as something we "often too readily" pin down on our clients. Casement addresses the importance of learning from the client, for instance, by implicit, often enacted criticism. In a similar vein to Hawkins and Shohet, Casement points out how the client's "mistakes" sometimes are an unconscious feedback to the therapist, a "mirroring" of her mistakes.

Casement refers to a therapist who brings his client's recent erratic attendance into supervision. Single loop learning may involve exploring this from a transference point of view, assuming that the client enacts a lack of trust and fear of commitment, and relives something from the past through the relationship with her therapist. The strategy involved would subsequently be to work towards an insight for the client about how her own behaviour, for instance, reproduces further disappointments. She could be argued, for instance, to be setting herself up for failure, so to speak, by making sure that she avoids a close relationship. This is by no means an irrelevant focus. However, as addressed by Sussman earlier, the intersubjective approach to therapy, the "two-person psychology" which has developed since Freud, requires new ways of exploring behaviours and reactions.

Casement explores different nuances within countertransference, which is where the therapist reacts to her client. Mirroring is a relatively uncomplicated, yet surprisingly neglected, way of assessing what is going on in the room. Casement's example below highlights our tendency to disregard our own infallibility. The example illustrates at the same time how double loop learning occurs when the therapist looks at a dilemma with his own impact in mind.

Example: the supervisee wants to explore the client's lateness as a problem linked to the client. He discloses at the same time being late himself to a session, and justifies this by feeling that he has compensated for this earlier, by extending their sessions. Casement explores this with reference to a dialogue in a group supervision.

> Let us take a few moments to consider the sequence here. The therapist might feel quite seriously threatened by the idea that his patient could be experiencing him as failing her . . . he could feel very vulnerable . . . [and] there he is, able to swing the problem away from himself . . . The patient has been telling him in so many different ways how shocked and disorientated she has been, because of his failure to be there at a proper time . . . This time it is she who is not there at the right time . . . *[T]his is what I mean by criticism by mirroring. The patient unconsciously enacts a version of the [therapist's] failure.* It is now she who gets the time wrong but it could be a way of holding up a mirror to him. [Casement, 2008b, p. 23, my italics]

The therapist's own resistance can, of course, be analysed from all sorts of angles. But the point raised in mirroring is to avoid being too ready to pathologize the client when a mismatch between explicit strategy and outcome occurs in therapy.

Our understanding of the therapist's own reactions is, within psychoanalytically inspired thinking, informed by theories on countertransference. Cashdan highlights the complexity as follows:

> Using the counter-transference means reaction to one's reaction. This means (1) allowing oneself to emotionally respond to the meta-communications embedded in the projective identification and (2) using this information as means of identifying the patient's pathology. It means that the therapist has to be willing to turn himself into an emotional barometer of sorts. The therapist needs to be emotionally responsible for what is taking place within himself as well as intellectually reflective regarding what is taking place in the relationship. [1988, pp. 101–102]

As addressed, there used to be the idea that a well-analysed therapist would be able to gain a conscious as clean and sterile as the hands of a surgeon: non-infectious and healthy. Countertransference was initially regarded as an indicator of the client's problems, as something that always came, was projected, from the client.

Clarkson points to an important distinction between "reactive" and "proactive" countertransference. She reserves the first category for responses originating in the client: "*Reactive countertransference* describes the reactions which are elicited by or induced in the psychoanalyst by the patient*" (Clarkson, 2002, p. 90). *Proactive countertransference* refers to feelings, atmospheres, projections, etc., which can be said to have been introduced by the psychotherapist herself.

Within psychoanalytic theory, Racker (2001) is a prominent voice in the area of transference and countertransference. Psychotherapy, agrees Racker, involves a fusion between the past and the present for both therapists and clients. Racker distinguishes between various types of countertransference: for instance, concordant and complementary countertransference.

This kind of thinking implies, as suggested before, that "the carrier of projections is not just any object but someone who offers a 'hook' to hang on" (Jung, in Sedgwick, 2005, p. 110).

Your reflection

Write one page maximum about your own personal input in a "tricky" situation.

Please take some time to consider a case where your own underlying personal material my have played a part in a "tricky" situation. If possible, write an example with the double loop learning model in mind.

- Consider a problem in your practice, perhaps a recurring one, small or large. It can be client time-keeping, contract conditions, cancellations policies, or whatever comes most readily to your mind right now.
- Think in terms of "mirroring" and describe how your own personal material may come into the equation.

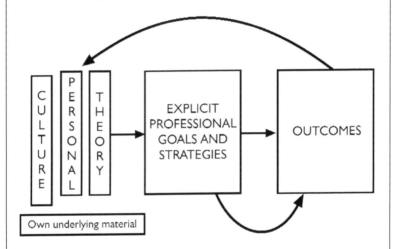

- Countertransference is an example of "framings" with which we can structure and understand such situations. What type of framing fits in with your modality? How does that work for you?

Reflexivity and double loop learning reach beyond the personal level of input. It encourages us also to challenge overly familiar professional frameworks and unaddressed political and cultural "framings".

Underlying theoretical framings

As Sussman implies earlier, it is reasonable to assume that therapists are prepared to address and "own" their own angle to the question "what brings me here?" An important question in this context is also *"what do I actually expect to do, as a therapist?"* Or, differently put, "how do I see my role?"

This question raises queries about what basic belief we generate knowledge from in the first place. What we hold as "evidence" (Cardinal, Hayward, & Jones, 2005, p. 11) is often based on "inference" from one set of beliefs to another. Inference is the "move that we make when we reason from one or more claims to a conclusion". This kind of thinking is usually referred to as an epistemological concern.

Epistemology derives from the Ancient Greek words "episteme", meaning "knowledge", and logos, meaning "rational". Epistemology is largely concerned with breaking down a potentially infinite ladder of beliefs and identifying patterns and structures in different inferences. Epistemology asks questions about the bedrock for beliefs. In our daily lives, knowledge holds a core position; it encompasses everything, from our assumption that morning will follow night to concerns of a moral, political, and religious nature. What we base our knowledge on is, therefore, of importance for us all. Taylor (2008, p. 88) writes,

> Epistemology concerns itself with knowledge generation and validation, meaning that it tries to ascertain how to make new knowledge and how to judge whether it is trustworthy and "true". Ontology is the meaning of human existence. These two main foci of human interest are related to each other if you accept the argument that knowing about human existence is the basis for knowing the answer to any questions humans might pose.

One important concern with regard to how we go about finding knowledge and evidence is what we actually see ourselves as working with in the first place. Do I regard therapy as a science or as an art? The truth may well be something in between an art and a science. In my book mentioned earlier (Bager-Charleson, 2010), counselling and psychotherapy is explored in terms of a dialectic relationship between art and science. However, Sussman's uncompromising conclusions are helpful when considering just how influential our basic belief about therapeutic practice can be. In the context of "benevolence" Sussman refers to a study of how therapy students perceive their professional future:

[T]he student who needs to identify with the role of an *absolute scientist* is usually one who needs to see himself as being powerful, masterful, intellectual, self-controlled and masculine, rejecting all traits of weakness, passivity and emotionality. [1992, p. 117]

Sussman quotes Hammer, who elaborated upon this distinction. Hammer found that the students who hoped to approach clients in the role of a scientist showed signs of "using the discipline of science as a means of exerting control . . . and deny an underlying conviction of weakness and vulnerability". At the other extreme, Hammer found student therapists who conceptualized their future therapeutic career as an art approached work with an air of altruism:

The student who strongly identifies with the role of an *absolute artist* . . . tends to try to gain a feeling of personal superiority by trying to confirm an image of himself as someone who is tender, gentle, affectionate, emotional, sensitive, intimate, noncombative, aesthetic, altruistic. [*ibid.*]

In both cases, Hammer found that the therapist placed him or herself on a pedestal, somehow leaving very little room to be anything but "perfect" and a saviour of a kind.

The debate about whether the "talking cure" actually is a cure is an ongoing one. Safran and Muran (1994, p. 223) write, "The tension between art and science is a perennial one, and any claims to have resolved this tension in a definite way would be trivializing a profoundly difficult issue".

Preaching and practising

When exploring practitioners' relationship to their professional frameworks, Argyris and Schön (1974, 1978) noted an interesting disparity between what people preached and what they actually practised. Their study implies a level of self-deception. Many practitioners regarded themselves as faithful to an espoused theory, while their actual theory-in-use could differ quite drastically from the professional framework by which they considered themselves informed.

A gap between an espoused theory, to which we officially adhere, and a theory-in-use can be indicated by signs of flexibility, openness, and, sometimes, maturity. An openness to the unique involved in all new client encounters is fundamental for reflective practice. The point here, however, is again to address underlying assumptions and the risk of making decisions on an uninformed basis.

Schön (1983) contends that professional strategies often are linked to our relationship to reality on several levels. His distinction between an *expert* stance and a *reflective* positioning resonates with our basic belief about reality. Do we see it as our role to show the client something that can be perceived as a "truth", deduced from a pre-fixed reality? Or is truth something that evolves between the client and her interaction with the world, both inside and outside the therapy room?

In their book *The Therapists' Use of Self*, Rowan and Jacobs write about three ways in which they see therapists positioning themselves. The therapist's position can be instrumental, authentic, or transpersonal:

> Each of these possibilities makes different assumptions about the self, about the relationship and about the level of consciousness involved in doing therapy. This, in turn, leads to different assumptions about the content of training and the process of supervision. [2002, p. 2]

Rowan and Jacobs pursued the idea of a marked difference between an espoused theory and a theory-in-use. On the face of it, they conclude, there are obvious stereotyped professional stances:

> Traditionally, the Freudian therapist has hidden behind the couch and been quite unknown to the client; the person-centred therapist has been consistently positive, speaking in warm tones, deeply empathizing with the client, repeating words and phrases with extra meaning; and the behavioural psychologist has a clipboard with a checklist of questions and carefully worked out instructions for exercises to be practiced now and outside session. [*ibid.*]

Rowan and Jacobs argue that therapists often interpret each modality in their different ways. They write,

> [However] within the same orientation each practitioner has developed ... a particular style, a way of being, a way of expressing themselves that is congruent with their approach, with the individual patient or client, and with his or her self. [*ibid.*]

As suggested earlier, Rowan and Jacobs define the therapists' different approaches in terms of an instrumental, authentic, and transpersonal stance:

> In the *instrumental position* the client is usually regarded as someone who has the problem, which needs to be put right . . . Specific techniques have to be learned and put into practice in time-limited work, for example, which nearly always include identification of a clear focus or problem. *The client is there to be cured* . . . More or better techniques are the way forward, and to test these objectively is the main goal of research . . . Working with the unconscious can be just as much part of this [*instrumental*] approach. It is equally possible here for the relationship to be long or short, close or distant, self-disclosing or anonymous, using transference or not, involving bodywork or not, political or not, humanistic, cognitive or emotive, or otherwise. The key thing is that . . . it is basically and I–it relationship . . .
>
> The *authentic* . . . therapist meets with and engages with the client additionally through attending to and experiencing what is going on within the therapist, through self-reflection, and monitoring her or his own feelings and thoughts. In the authentic way of being, personal involvement is much more acceptable, with the therapist much more closely identified with the client and more openly concerned to explore the therapeutic relationship. The idea of *the wounded healer* is often mentioned as is the idea of *personal growth* . . .
>
> In the *transpersonal way of being*, the boundaries between therapist and client may fall away. Both may occupy the same space at the same time, at the level of what is sometimes termed *"soul"*, sometimes "heart" and sometimes "essence": what they have in common is a willingness to let go of all aims and all assumptions. [*ibid.*, p. 6, my italics]

Each approach involves, in other words, a different stance to the relationship between therapist and client. And these relationships relate, in turn, to what the therapist expects therapy to contribute.

As suggested in the introduction, Guggenbuhl-Craig contends that priests, social workers, psychotherapists, and other practitioners within the "helping" professions are equipped with an exclusive "right" to make judgements about what is "good" for others. On what grounds, asks Guggenbuhl-Graig?

[A]ctions must [sometimes] be taken against the client's will, since he is [presumed] not capable of recognizing what is good for him. Under certain circumstances the [practitioner] has legal means to execute such measures on the basis of his *own judgement* ... [Guggenbuhl-Craig, 2009, p. 17]

The term *judgement* has an epistemological meaning, addressed as early as 1781, by the philosopher Immanuel Kant. He examined the collectively held assumption at the time that only God, ultimately, understood the meaning and order of life. At the time, there was a budding oppositional view advocating what would eventually become the Darwinistic revolution, suggesting that Man, not God, was the almighty and knew the truth. Kant, at a very early stage, stepped in between, and sensed the dilemma with which nowadays social and human sciences grapple, which is, can I actually find any "off the cuff" rules, any "two-plus-two-makes-four" rules, as Guggenheim-Craig puts it, in my profession? Our references in this book to reflective practice, constructivism, and constructionism could be argued to have been addressed as early as 1781, when Kant grapples with the dilemma of what we base our basic belief on, and subsequently generate our knowledge and "evidence". Kant wrote,

There can be no doubt that all our knowledge begins with experience ... As no representation, except when it is an intuition, relates immediately to its object, no concept is ever referred to as an object immediately, but some other representation of it ... Judgement is therefore the mediate knowledge of an object, that is the representation of a representation of it. In every judgement we find a concept holding for many representations. [2007, pp. 39, 97]

Your reflection

- Consider for a while the concept of basic beliefs, and the idea that they may be shifting, almost optional.
- The three different relationships suggested by Rowan and Jacobs could all be said to hold different basic beliefs about reality, the way that we interact, and make sense of our reality. Allow yourself some time to consider where you stand with regard to this. What differs the authentic, instrumental, and transpersonal stance, do you think?

- Allow some time to consider the implications of each "stance" towards the client. Picture a therapist with one particular stance in mind. Write about the therapist in I-form, that is, as if the narrator is the therapist.
- Write uninterrupted for ten minutes, continuing from the following sentence:

  "I watched the client attend to a speck of dust on the left sleeve; after a moment's silence, I said . . ."

Underlying cultural assumptions

The neo-Freudian Jacques Lacan represents a new thinking on counselling and psychotherapy, linked to post-structuralist and post-modern theories. Like Freud, Lacan has contributed considerably to the debate about what actually constitutes talking therapies. Both Lacan and Freud have referred to therapy as an "impossible profession" (Freud, 1937) in their different ways. Lacan writes about the "untenable position of the analyst" (1990, in Nobus, 2000), but approaches the dilemma from a slightly different angle than Freud, who never ceased to strive for certainties. Lacan assumes that we can never fully understand another person; we are doomed to filter each other's messages through our own framing mechanisms. Even the silence is interpreted. "I always speak the truth. Not the whole truth, because there is no way to say it all. Saying it all is literally impossible. Yet it is through this very impossibility that the truth holds onto the real" (Lacan, in Nobus, 2000, p. 92).

Lacan argues that scientific reasoning rests on different basic beliefs than what psychotherapy does.

This puts the therapist in a more equal position to the client. It suggests that our interpretations *always* may be challenged and questioned. Freud's comparison of the analyst to an archaeologist assumed that there were tangible, albeit buried, pieces of "evidence" to reveal. Lacan's thinking involves a postmodern critique of the prior thinking of experts and pre-fixed "evidences". Human and social sciences are different from natural sciences. Human sciences revolve around people's meaning-making processes. Polkinghorne (1988) addresses how therapy revolves more around "narrative truths" than "historical truth". The "truth", in terms of what matters to the client's life, does not so much revolve around the actual event as to what meanings we attach to the events. Constructivist and postmodern thinking highlight, as suggested earlier, how knowledge is "co-created between therapist and client"—even our silence "speaks", as Lacan points out. Postmodern thinking focuses our attention on narratives and language, often with reference to culturally available ways of relating to things. Mitchell (2002) compares, for instance, Freud and the early psychoanalysts' way of referring to women with the oppression of a social class, barred from access to power and cited as proof of inferiority. Billig (1997, p. 1) writes, "Scholars have debated whether psychoanalytic ideas should be rejected outright for their masculine assumptions . . . These debates have led feminist scholars to look at the famous case-studies in new ways . . .".

As suggested, double loop learning helps to expand our analytical frame "beyond the obvious" to explicitly identify and challenge underlying cultural, personal, and theoretical assumptions. As an example, Freud's famous case study *Fragment of an Analysis of a Case of Hysteria* can, with hindsight, be compared to what Argyris and Schön (1978) refer to as a "single loop" learning. In one of his case studies, Freud rationalizes his client Dora's repulsions of her father's friend's approaches as a symptom of "repressed" sexuality and Oedipal wishful fantasies. Postmodern writers, post-feminist in particular, highlight how Freud constructs Dora's problem as linked to her own suppressed sexuality. This "cause and effect" thinking about hysteria reflects a set of expectations about not only women in society at the time, but also Freud's own personal assumptions. Billig's (1997) critique of Freud's case expresses this shift in framing:

> Freud's role in the saga is being reassessed. He no longer appears as a passive listener and detached scientist . . . In the late twentieth century, the problem is no longer seen to be Dora's resistance to the male phallus, but has become Freud's assumption about women's desire . . . [p. 1]

A reflexive awareness would involve, as Carter and Gradin (2001, p. 4) say, "trying on the perspective, the world view of an 'other' for long enough to look back critically at ourselves, our ideas, our assumptions". Double loop thinking turns, in this sense, the problem back to the assessor, or the so-called "knower", and encourages questions such as, "how do I know?" "What assumptions may influence my understanding of the 'problem'?" "What alternative views could I take?"

Mental health practitioners enjoy a tremendous power through their assessments of "sane" and "insane", rights and wrongs, thinkable and unthinkable. These are powerful narratives that can result in confinement for some and ordain others with divine status, depending on time and place. Many "diagnoses", asserts Foucault, rest on moral and social values rather than "medical facts". Our thinking and our experiences are "shaped" by what Foucault proposes as a "repertoire of dominant narratives". Historic documents reflecting, for instance, male doctors' perception of female clients' problems lend distressing illustrations of how emotions and stereotypical images are intertwined, for instance with regard to the "diagnose" of "hysteria". In Foucault's *Madness and Civilisation* (Foucault, 1984), he explores, for instance, mental health "care" with reference to how a young girl is hospitalized:

> [she was] treated with great gentleness [for showing a certain "haughtiness" which could not be tolerated at the asylum]; she spoke "of her parents with nothing but bitterness". It was decided to subject her to a regime of strict authority; the keeper, "in order to tame this inflexible character, seized the moment of the bath and expressed himself forcibly concerning certain unnatural persons who dared oppose their parents and disdain their authority . . . she was henceforth soothed and could not sufficiently express her gratitude toward the keeper who had brought an end to her continual agitation, and had restored tranquillity and calmed her heart". [pp. 160–161].

An egalitarian view of the therapeutic relationship

The question of why we choose to be a therapist opens, in this sense, further questions, for instance, with regard to what we expect to do as therapists; what we believe our role as therapists will entail.

The "helping" professions play an important role on a cultural and political level. Post-structuralists such as Foucault alert us to how "sanity" and "illness" are relative, socially constructed concepts (Gergen, 2009), and that therapists need to shoulder their responsibility in terms of how society values, dismisses, includes, and excludes people. The feminist critique of Freud's interpretation of women is one example of how dominating narratives can work. Intercultural theory lends us further valuable insights regarding inclusion and exclusion. We feel that the latter is a still markedly absent voice in today's therapeutic discourse. For that reason, we have reserved some extra space for intercultural aspects. For Sherna, underlying cultural values and beliefs play a significant role in both how she came to be a therapist and with regard to how she practises today. Her case study will highlight this and involves further references to intercultural theory.

We have all approached the question about why we have chosen to be therapists with reflective practice in mind. Our aim has always been to take the question "why" as earnestly and seriously as we can. This involves an attempt to consider the issue both in light of our personal history and our theoretical and socio-cultural values and assumptions. This puts us in a similar situation to our clients, as Sussman proposes; the focus is not only on actual events, but on the meaning that we have attached to them and how we have applied the experiences to our practice. Therapists are, in this sense, no longer a homogenous group of "experts". Like our clients, everything that we do will be tainted by "the human factor". Like our clients, our understanding of the world is constructed in the sense that Safran and Muran (2003) address below. They describe the constructivist thinking as "cultural shift towards a postmodern sensibility". They continue,

This shift has a number of important therapeutic implications. One of the most important is that it challenges the traditional view that the therapist has some privileged understanding of reality . . . *It is thus consistent with a more egalitarian view of the therapeutic relationship* . . . this *involves becoming aware of our preconceptions and the way in which they currently shape our understanding* . . . [p. 56]

Your reflection

The social constructionist perspective can be useful when considering what impact society has on our lives. It is linked to what we earlier described as critical reflexivity.

In his book about social constructionism, Gergen (2009, p. 2) suggests "What we take to be true about the world largely depends on how we approach it, and how we approach it depends on the social relationships of which we are a part . . .".

As we will explore later on, in Sheila's story in particular, even emotions can be traced to our "enmeshment" in society.

- Write about the ways in which gender, ethnicity, or religion might have shaped your attitude about yourself. Focus, for instance, on a time when the stereotypical expectation about your gender, ethnicity, or religion seemed to contrast with your own "inner" realities and view about yourself.

CHAPTER FOUR

Sofie's story: growing up with mental illness in the family

Introduction

I n the following six chapters, each of the members of the reflective writing group will reflect on our own reasons for being a therapist.

The process of *reflection* involves examining our experiences and assessing what is "real".

My cycle of reflection

The story that I tell here has been difficult to pin down. Stories usually are. I am at the stage of rewriting. I have scribbled and researched. There are notes from uninterrupted writing and quotes from reading which have triggered new ideas, documented in my "dialectical" notebook. All this has now got to come together. When organizing events into a certain order, which "telling" really is about, I have focused on organizing events in a way that puts what I have *learnt* in the forefront. I have a particular "crisis" in mind, which I regard as something of a turning point. It highlights both what brought me into a career in therapy in the first place, and also illustrates how my assumptions about my role as a therapist needed to be reassessed. So, what happened, and what came out of it?

I have found earlier that my own way of thinking and exploring things follows what seems to be a common cycle of reflection. In the previously mentioned book about reflective practice (Bager-Charleson, 2010), I gathered different theories which seemed to point to similar themes in the way we work through problems. I decided to call it the "Act-model". I have used its "steps" as headings in my story about Andy and "his wife". The Act-model stands for

- *acknowledging* a problem in terms of bits of unconnected information, which have no organization and make no sense;
- *considering* the situation on a "unistructural" level, by simple and obvious connections, without any real sense of the significance, that is, not sure what it means;
- *connecting* on a "multistructural" level, where a number of connections may be made, but the meta-connections between them are missed, as is their significance for the whole;
- *transforming* on a "relational" level, where a sense of the significance of the parts in relation to the whole emerges;
- *transforming* on an extended abstract level, where connections are made not only within the given subject area, but also beyond it. We begin to generalize about the problem, put into the context of other situations, and transfer principles and ideas underlying the specific instance into other contexts.

Andy and "his wife", and I

By the time I meet Andy and his wife, Jane, I am in my second year of training at Relate. I have always been interested in the mind. I feel well equipped to work with relationships and psychological issues since I come from a broken home myself, and have learnt to look after my father, who suffered from manic depression.

Andy and Jane's presented problem is how to deal with an affair that Andy had a year ago. Andy is a floor layer and Jane works part time as a shop assistant in the local supermarket. Their relationship "went tits up when the kids came along", as Andy put it. He speaks fondly about their two children, but keeps coming back to that it is in everyone's interest that they separate.

"I don't want to hurt anyone", repeats Andy. "But I'm just not cut out for this family thing!"

Andy is friendly, and gets very emotional. I find him endearing. Jane striked me as patient, almost maternal.

"I hear what you are saying, love", he tells me in our third session, "I appreciate what you're trying to do, I really do. But nah, it's just not for me, I'm the kind of fellow who's better off in the old bed-sit." He smiles. I smile back.

I catch a glimpse of Jane as she reaches for the tissues;

"But you promised," she says, and blows her nose. Loudly. I want to tell her not to. Andy looks at her, tapping with his right foot to a beat, as I have noticed him doing before when agitated.

"You said you would try," whispers Jane into her tissue.

"I mean, what can I say?" exclaims Andy and raises his hands in defeat. "I am a bastard and that's my whole point. I'm trying to help you out here! You don't want to grow old with someone like me."

"You're not trying . . ."

"Ah, for God's sake, you know how we're going to end up!"

"You always say that . . . I'm not your like mum, I'm nothing like her. You're trying to make it into like we're like your parents . . ." cries Jane.

Andy looks out of the window, seeming to be lost in thought, while Jane continues crying.

"It is horrible when the parents don't get on," he reflects, still looking out of the window, and adds, "It does your head in."

"But we're not like them," repeats Jane.

Andy's mother was, by all accounts, a "cruel" mother. Andy refuses to talk about it: "It's too horrible to even think about." Jane tries to comfort him, and the contrast between the inconsiderate, unloving mother and Jane becomes obvious in the room. When addressed, Andy admits to the difference, but remains convinced about the inevitability of their destiny.

"I want to get out before it's too late. I just want to run to a little bed-sit so that no one gets hurt."

My hypothesis and "espoused theory"

Ever since our first session, I have worked with a psychodynamically informed hypothesis about Andy predicting an evil outcome on the basis of his previous negative experiences. I am wondering why he is so keen to perceive himself as a hopeless partner. Where does this idea of self as bad come from? Jane evidently loves him, keeps telling him that reality is different to what his worst fears tell him. *I* can see that he is a good man, underneath. *Why* can't he see it?

I discuss the issue with my supervisor. I have dug out a paper by Winnicott about "clinical fear of breakdown". My supervisor seems surprised.

"You've been working very hard with all your cases, you really seem to take this seriously."

I find that comment strange. Why shouldn't I, I wonder? I am beginning to wonder if I will be able to trust my supervisor; is she beginning to encourage me to become disinterested?

Not expecting much of an input from my supervisor, I proceeded with my hypothesis about what Winnicott (1974) refers to as a compulsive need to repeat a past experience in the hope of reconnecting and repairing the "original failure in the facilitating environment".

People can, suggests Winnicott, have lived through traumatic events without yet having *experienced* them. The "absolute dependency" of the child prevents him or her from acknowledging, "taking in", the damage inflicted by their parent. This resonates with what Miller (1997) concludes, that until the damage has been acknowledged, confronted, and mourned, the adult will remain "imprisoned" with an eternal sense of pending danger, a "nameless dread", re-enacting the event again and again. The couple therapist Cleavely (1993) writes,

> perhaps it is not so much what happens to us as children that is so significant to future development, but *how* what happens is managed—whether there is someone there to catch you. Part of the

purpose, perhaps, behind the compulsive need to repeat a past experience . . . is to get in touch with the "original failure in the facilitating environment" (Winnicott 1974) and from there to discover a better way of managing it. [p. 58]

My understanding of the case is, in this sense, guided by the psychoanalytically inspired focus on projective identifications of "split-off" and denied feelings. I believe that Andy projects split-off emotions and fears based on an early object relationship on to his wife. There is, to my mind, a kind of cause and effect. If old fears and fantasies about relationships are revealed, the relationship between Andy and Jane will improve (Figure 6).

"You always call her Andy's wife . . .," reflects my supervisor back to me during our session. Again, I leave feeling misunderstood; can she not see how it was in Jane's own interest that Andy reconstructed his meaning of himself? Does she not realize that the direct focus on Andy would help Jane enormously, *indirectly*?

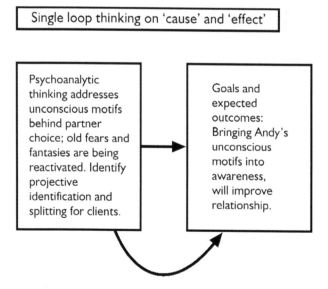

Figure 6. Single loop, cause and effect thinking on the problem (Bager-Charleson 2010).

Acknowledging that something is "wrong"

Sometimes, problems sneak up on us. Both Casement (2008b) and Sedgwick (2005) write about a creeping "sense of guilt" which alerts them that something is "wrong". For instance, when sensing that, as Casement (2008b, p. 154) puts it, "an intrusive element from the analyst provides a focus that has not been initiated by the patient". The therapist has, in other words, fed the agenda with his or her own issues.

My creeping sense of something being wrong at this stage comes with a sense of "jetlag" after each session of couple counselling, not just with Andy and his wife, but with my two other couples, too; John and Philip "and their wives". The women are so passive, invisible, and often leave me frustrated. I return home feeling disconnected and detached from my surroundings; still revved up, somehow, and alone with an experience that I would not know where to begin to explain.

"It sounds both frustrating and very *special*," reflects my therapist, during one of our sessions where I have talked about the impact that work seems to have on me. I have told her about feeling tense and unable to relax and have tried to convey the feelings I carried of great responsibility.

It will, however, take a considerable number of nightmares and a period of excessive eating and drinking before I begin to consider the female clients and my reactions as a "problem". In supervision, I am confronted once again.

"I don't get any sense of presence of Jane in the room," reflects my supervisor. "What does Jane want in all this?"

That same night, I dream about abandoning Jane in an airport. She is in a wheelchair, and I leave her in the toilets to help Andy catch a plane.

"Helping Andy to catch a plane . . .," reflects my therapist in our subsequent session.

"I had this feeling of helping Jane indirectly, I was doing it for her . . ." I reply.

"For her . . .?"

"Well, yes, and for me . . . it was really urgent; if I didn't get Andy on the plane the whole place might explode," I explain.

My therapist lapses into silence. Eventually, she says, "The whole world would fall apart?"

It hits me at this point how my own fears and fantasies had been brought into the relationship with Andy and Jane. Jane "is" my mother; the mother I often "killed off", dismissed, and rejected in my quest to "save" my father from losing his mind. I have been hypersensitive to everything Jane did that could provoke Andy to distance himself further. Jane has "allowed" it to happen. She grew up in the shadow of a schizophrenic brother. We meet fleetingly, without acknowledging each other in our own rights, in a place where "keeping others sane" is at the forefront of our minds. We may have developed different strategies, different defences to cope, but I am beginning to recognize that we share fears.

Considering and connecting

Argyris and Schön (1974) introduced the term "theories-in-use" to highlight the impact that implicit beliefs can have on our strategies. The espoused theory refers to rational, explicit objectives to which we openly and officially commit. Our theory-in-use, on the other hand, which is what we actually end up doing, often rests on underlying, tacit assumptions and beliefs based on what we take for granted or have learnt to ignore, maybe even deny. I resist for as long as I can acknowledging what impact my underlying assumptions of being an "omnipotent" helper can have on the work. At this stage of the work, I am beginning to feel thoroughly deskilled. The disconnected feeling I had before was tinted with a sense of excitement; I was a woman on a mission, feeling "special", as my therapist had observed. My single loop thinking on Andy and Jane felt somehow "safe"; it kept me feeling in control of things. Perhaps I would have been able to stay within this frame for longer had it not been for my supervisor and therapist. The creeping sense of guilt could have been kept at bay; there are plenty of escape routes apart from eating and drinking too much.

The biggest problem for me was my own underlying ambivalence towards receiving help; it put me in a vulnerable position. I am beginning to recognize how my sense of self is tied to self-sufficiency.

"It is a strategy developed for a reason", as my therapist would say. It had become a wall around me, where every brick involved an experience of disillusion accompanied by a lot of pain.

Having caught a glimpse of the underlying personal assumptions that had an impact on the work, there seemed to be no return. I am aware of the value of personal therapy for psychotherapists, but I am unprepared for what deep-seated effects challenging the "helper" role actually have when your whole identity has been based on being one.

This becomes a turning point with regard to expanding the framework into what Schön would call a double loop learning.

Personal underlying assumptions in my theory-in-use

On one level, of course, addressing old patterns is deeply rewarding. It is like taking off a pair of sunglasses; things are generally much brighter when you do not expect a particular accident to happen all the time. It is a relief to be reminded of another world than my fears and fantasies have told me to expect. I am surprised and relieved by seeing Jane as a person in her own right. She quickly begins to fill the room once "given" the space.

Altering my own agenda affects not only the work with Jane and Andy, but affects my couple work as a whole. The men seem to "take less space" in the room and the women become more vocal: Jane flourishes in particular. Her growth proceeds until one session when she surprises me with her elaborate plans about further education and a new career. She says that she has reached a decision that "enough is enough".

"I'm am ready to move on, I have had enough of "Andy's whims" and changing wishes," she smiles, and continues, "I didn't see how manipulative Andy could be until I saw him here, with you," she says calmly and in an almost maternal way. I feel pitied.

Managing change

Experiencing loss is often an inevitable part of reflective learning, as Roffey-Barentsen and Malthouse (2009, p. 20) write in the section about "managing change": "[W]hen reflecting, you will encounter change . . . *you will have lost an element that made up a part of what you were*" [my italics].

Trying on new perspectives necessarily involves a questioning of one's own previous ways of acting and being. There comes the inevitable point when we look critically on past strategies, and, at this point, everything to date can seem wrong, futile, and inadequate. In my case, being a "helper" needed to be reassessed; being a helper and a support to my father was a role around which I had built my life.

The session with Jane triggers a real sense of lack of self-belief. I feel deskilled, lost, and very afraid. The sense of anxiety follows me wherever I go, at home and at work. I even found myself shaking one day when reading the newspaper. It is as if all the horrors in the world jump out at me. The world seems like a thoroughly scary place in which I lack all sense of control.

"I am wondering what you want from supervision," says my supervisor the next time we meet. I struggle to talk about Jane's reaction. I want to return to my old focus on Andy, who I fear is about to leave Jane. "So what?" said my supervisor. "Why would that be so bad?"

On the way home I burst into tears in the car.

"Do you think that you enacted something from your work in the supervision . . . something about feeling totally alone with the responsibility?" asks my therapist the next time we meet. I have told her about the eerie feeling I have had in my stomach and about how the world looks on a cold winter's day—almost as you look at it on a picture. I try to comfort myself by talking about our painter at home.

"His dog just died. He's an army man, but when he told me about it he started to cry."

"People do that with you," reflects my therapist. I feel momentarily pleased with myself; people can come to me with their problems. I am, after all, strong.

"I think it is that they recognize something in you . . . something about *your* loss."

When I hear my therapist saying "your loss", something shifts inside me, breaks down, and I cry. I hear myself sobbing; I sound like a wounded animal.

Connecting and making sense

The simple world "loss", uttered with reference to me by a woman who I feel is on "my side", works like a key to my own locked cupboard, or to what Miller (1997, p. 20) would call my "inner prison". This kind of prison is secured, guarded by ourselves, to keep the "intense emotional world of early childhood" at bay. An escape, says Miller, involves giving up what has constituted ourselves since as long as we can bear to remember. Breaking free involves confronting the "mourning aroused by our parent's failure to fulfil our primary needs". A fugitive will have to face "the reality that s/he perhaps never was loved as a child for what s/he was but was instead needed and exploited for his or her achievements . . .".

Accepting this notion of myself and my childhood requires tapping into the dream which I think that I always shared with my father, about him being well enough to care about matters outside the mist which eventually would consume him completely. Aldridge and Becker (2003) write that children and their mentally ill parents sometimes enjoy a stronger and more intense bond than people in "normal" families do. "Enjoy" is perhaps not the right word. And the idea of an intense bond beckons idealization and glorification, which is always tempting in a family where reality simply is not enough. Still, mourning my father and my own partly lost childhood involved experiencing both pain and joy. I had a caring, loving and loyal mother, but allowed myself now to immerse myself in memories shared by my "mad dad" and me. I use this expression in the fondest possible way, because it brings me as close to the truth as I can get with regard to how it was between us. My father's mental illness did bring out another side to him as a father, and he was, in this respect, my "mad dad". For good and for bad, my father invited me into his mist; I had a free pass and moved in and out of "his" world as naturally as a child moves between parents in different countries or continents. In his mist there existed much pain, disappointment, and agony. But there was also the Boogie-woogie, which he played on the piano, and the African dancing we performed on outings, be it in the forest, in shops, or at the nursery when he picked me up at the end of the day, or at grandma's during a too-formal dinner. There was, above all, the endless jumping in waves. For hours and hours, until I became too self-conscious to do so, did we play together in the Baltic sea. The latter encapsulates perhaps my fondest memories of my father. We came alive in the water. My father would toss me up in the air again and again and again, until I stopped asking to be tossed any more. He would jump with me through the waves until I told him that I had "run out of jumps". In spite of seven years of personal therapy, these memories still make me want to weep and need to stop, sit, and stay with the loss. Gone. My father is gone. He has been gone in many ways ever since I laid my eyes on him; the stable, reliable father-father was simply never there—only in my stubborn dreams. But my "mad dad" was there, maybe not as much *for* me as *with* me until he died from liver cancer.

From that, I began to mourn my father and my childhood in therapy, I settle for the fact that my father was a man who *wanted* to love. But I am also connecting with anger, and realize at this stage how hard I always worked to earn his love. His love was often, as Miller puts it, "conditional", and I could not rely on him to protect or look after me. In connection with the therapy, I begin to read, think, feel, and talk about what it is like to be a child with a mentally ill parent. I recognize in myself what Aldridge and Becker (2003, p. 58) call "precocious competence" and "parentification". I identify with what they write about the child caring for their parent "at the expense of their own developmentally appropriate needs and pursuits". I feel crippled for a while, and suggest that we discontinue the therapy; I have my own children to think of, I tell my therapist. I cannot afford to "sink too deep". In response, my therapist suggests meeting twice weekly, and I return from our session feeling furious. I cancel our next session. I begin to eat and drink too much again, and into the second week I recognize that I feel only half alive; I feel sluggish, tired, and have got a hangover. We are in the process of deciding on a family holiday, and I am dreading it. In fact, I find that I dread most things. It is on my return to the therapist that I realize that I have slipped back into my "inner prison" again. I also recognize how this time I want to get out. I am heading towards my fortieth birthday and I do not want to dread living any longer.

Dropping out

At this stage, the reader may wonder what happened with my clients. It is worth noting that during some of the low points referred to above, my supervisor commended me highly for sensitive work. When listening, for instance, to an audio recorded session, as part of the training, my supervisor compliments me on my ability to "read the emotional temperature in the room"; "It is like listening to a pianist playing really difficult scales without effort. I think you have got a real talent for this," she says.

I do not return home "revved up" and excited as I would do earlier after a "good session". It feels now rather as if I have been able to lift something really heavy because I have been forced to develop certain muscles, and that I sometimes almost cannot stop myself from using them, almost like twitching automatically. The supervision session also reminds me of how bad I have been at living my own life; I worry about living through others.

Jane and Andy decided to stay together, but both of them seemed greatly changed towards the end of our work. Jane did pursue her new training and new career, and Andy's role in the household changed drastically from something marginal to a real hands-on father.

Once I completed my training at Relate, however, I decided to stop working as a couple counsellor. I am beginning to recognize that I do not have to help other people as a living, and the idea feels liberating. I recognize a certain value in my muscles, or what Miller would call antennae, but I need time to consider whether I *want* to use them.

Abstracting and transforming new meanings into action

It takes me quite a while to come around to the decision that I actually want to pursue a career as a therapist. When I do, I return with a new appetite for learning. I am beginning to sense the value of my earlier experience in a new way. I no longer feel like a compulsive helper. It is almost a question of "recycling" experiences; I am keen to learn from my own and others' mistakes and experiences and to "use" them again, so to speak, in a new and different context. This should not be confused with displacing and disowning. To reuse waste, you need to sort through it, carefully. You need to arrange it in different piles and consider what can be of use where. This next stage of my career reminds me of this kind of process.

I know that I need to learn more about the therapeutic relationship, and this guides me into further training. I undertake training that lends me an integrative perspective on my own practice. I adopt, for instance, another view on countertransference. With my own experiences in mind, it makes sense to assume that counter-transference is so much more than only what Freud originally proposed in terms of a "means of identifying the patient's pathol-ogy". I begin to read Racker's (2001) fascinating text on the different forms of countertransference, and I find that I agree with Clarkson's (2002) distinction between reactive and proactive countertransfer-ence. It seems obvious, now, that the therapist never ceases to be a human being and, as a consequence, brings his or her own material into the room. On my training for an MSc in psychoanalytic, exis-tential, and postmodern theory on counselling and psychotherapy, I am given the opportunity to compare some very different "fram-ings" of the therapeutic relationship. We are encouraged to engage in the views dialectically. By "dialectical engagement", I mean moving back-and-forth between opposing ideas, where differing assumptions, ideas, and ways of seeing things are pitted against each other. By adopting an opposite stance and by trying to under-stand the other person's views, our own beliefs and assumptions are made explicit. We can "loop back" our assumptions from a more critical stance. This brings you, curiously, often back to the same point, yet with a very different understanding of it.

For instance, I still often work with projective identification and split-off emotions from earlier relationships in mind, particularly in couple work. The core of the previously referred to single and double loop thinking has, in this sense, not been dismissed and replaced, as such. Yet, as soon as you engage in the strategy with underlying assumptions in mind, the strategies become impossible to treat as "fixed entities". On the basis of my own experiences, I tend to agree with the Jungian analyst Sedgwick, who suggests that the therapist accepts that countertransference "inevitably residues with one's own wounds". For a projection to latch on, there needs to be a "hook" in the first place, continues Sedgwick, and quotes Jung (2005, p. 108), "The carrier of projections is not just any object, but someone who offers a 'hook' to hang on".

Like Miller, he warns of the "Quack" who "falls into his shadow of omnipotence", believing himself to be divine and ultimately rely-ing on the patient to carry all pathology. The Quack needs the client to own strong emotions: "The analyst caught in the shadow . . .

stops living his own life altogether . . . The patients live, love and suffer for him" (p. 25).

My shadow came to the forefront during supervision, when the three-way collusion was brought to my awareness. The way that Jane lacked confidence, together with Andy's mood swings, fitted particularly well into my own blueprints. It was a scenario that felt familiar, and one that had brought me into to take up therapy as a career for many wrong reasons. I have tried to capture the process of the reflective learning that I felt took place in the model below. The previous single loop thinking expanded in light of issues raised in supervision about my own underlying assumptions (Figure 7). Personal therapy, peer groups, ongoing supervision, and continuous professional development (CPD), spurred me to consider the problem in a new light and offered new connections. Acknowledging, connecting, and transforming are, in this sense, part of an ongoing cycle, particularly perhaps in a profession always in the emotional firing line.

Reflective practice

The difference between reflective learning and reflective practice is the focus on how the learning feeds into, and affects, the practice. The ACT model illustrates thinking which starts with acknowledging a "mismatch" between intentions and outcome, and where the strategy comes under scrutiny with an interest in outside influences. In my case, my own personal assumptions crept in. With the lenses that I was wearing, I saw my parents rather than clients. When examining the reflective learning cycle, Lehman refers to transformation in different ways. Emotions, basic values, and strategies are interwoven concerns:

> Often the process of transformation takes place within ourselves, together with the development of awareness of what constrains or pushes us to feel and act in the way we do. Adjustments to beliefs or values may occur due to this awareness. [2008, p. 208]

Transformation, continues Lehman, involves a "sense of ownership" of both assets and limitations:

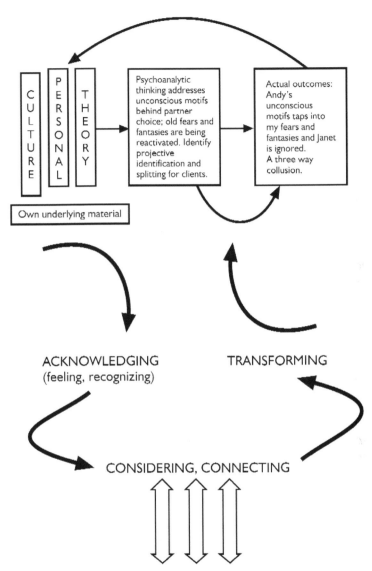

Figure 7.

The transformation process includes the realization of multiple truths and perspectives for every situation and brings into consciousness the choices that are made in the process of interpreting live experiences . . . [W]e develop a sense of ownership for what lies within our repertoire of professional actions. [*ibid.*]

The transformation invariably feeds into practice and changes its direction and outcome. I look at this as a form of ongoing recycling of old, useless, and sometimes dysfunctional aspects of ourselves and our experiences. Our own therapy, CPD, peer groups, and supervision are assets at hand for our attempts to turn "dysfunctional" aspects into something potentially valuable. This thinking seems to me to be captured in Sedgwick's contention below about getting to know, finding out about, and using one's, at times, potential "pathology", in new and other ways:

> from a Jungian perspective a "wounded healer" does not mean a "once wounded—now recovered" one, but one who is currently vulnerable as well . . . Accordingly, analysts need not try to eliminate their pathology, but *know it and utilize it*. [Sedgwick, 2005, p. 112]

To become eventually involved in reflective practice seems now like a natural development of my personal relationship to ambivalence. Chaos and excessive reflection come as a pair, in my world, incompatible yet inseparable. Writing about reflective practice is, in this sense, an example of where I have "recycled" problems, experiences, and what could be called a "pathology", or, at least, certainly "wounds", into something potentially useful. *Transformative learning*, where problems and experiences are reflected upon and eventually put into practice again, is, to my mind, an ongoing process. Reflective learning, as referred to in my own ACT-model of events, involves a kind of cycle that comes into use whenever a new problem occurs. I believe that problems surface all the time, in life in general, but in our profession in particular.

Your reflection

- Write about a crisis at work. Begin with a moment where you sensed, felt, or realized that something was "wrong". You decide the meaning of "wrong". Perhaps you reacted with dreams, sadness, or hyperactivity? Eating, overeating, or other means of displacement or enactments? Trace a significant reaction for you, concentrate on putting that into words, and let your story about yourself and your work evolve freely from there.

Recommended reading

Symington, N. (1986). *The Analytic Experience. Lectures from the Tavistock.* London: Free Association Books.

Psychotherapy "can not be taught", is how Symington begins his book. He writes, "I can describe it, I can lead you to it, but you have to experience the reality of it". This is a highly recommended book, where psychotherapy is explained without the mystery of it being lost.

McLeod, J. (2003). *Doing Counselling Research.* London: Sage.

I recommend this book to people who want to learn more about research, perhaps get a "taster" to demystify the idea of writing about and researching your own practice.

CHAPTER FIVE

Sheila's story: how meanings emerge between people

I came to the world of therapy relatively late in life. When I was forty, I was working in a senior position in Home Care, and I became aware that I was eating chocolate to cope with the stresses that this job brought. When I sought the help of a dietician, she recommended a therapist who specialized in issues of emotional eating. My therapist helped me to look at my relationship to food, and how this was related to my life's experiences. My mother had died suddenly of cancer when I was ten years old. This was in the 1950s, when cancer and death were, to some extent, considered to be taboo subjects, and I do not think that anyone had the language to help me to understand what was happening. After my mother died, I was told not to worry, and that my father and brother would look after me. My mother was never discussed at home again, and, as it was beyond my friends' experience, it was difficult to have the conversation with them either. In those days, counselling was not readily available, and I was left to manage as best I could. My family had never talked freely about their emotions; in fact, they never talked freely about anything. My parents' marriage had broken down, but, as divorce was not so commonplace then, they had decided to stay together.

My parents were not sociable people, and I was often told not to talk about certain issues, for example, my brother's eczema. As a child I was confused about what I was permitted to say outside the family, and so I suppose I erred on the side of caution and talked very little. Hence, I came to be seen as shy. My therapist helped me to make connections beween what was happening in the present with what had happened in the past. During the process of my own personal therapy, I became very intrigued with the practice, and this contributed to my desire to train as a therapist myself.

My therapy had also helped me to see that life was too short to get stuck in ruts, and that it was important to follow your passions. During my social work training, I spent some time working in a large, Victorian psychiatric hospital, and I was involved with patients who had spent many years of their life in this institution. I also worked with the acute psychiatric services at the local hospital, and so it was possible to contrast different types of care. It was through this experience that I developed an affinity to mental health. Although I had returned to Home Care after qualifying as a social worker, I decided to reconsider my career and sought a job in the field of mental health.

While I was working as a mental health social worker, I was encouraged to take further training in counselling or psychotherapy, and so I took this opportunity. I chose systemic/family therapy, as these ideas were very prevalent in the social services department where I worked, and I was influenced by how the communication within families could have an impact on an individual. The training and skills I developed through systemic/family therapy greatly enhanced my abilities to work with clients suffering from mental health issues, and it was extremely rewarding to contribute to the restoration of a client's well-being.

Systemic/family therapy is a relatively new therapy, which emerged in the 1950s. Rather than locating problems within individuals, family therapists became interested in the interactions that went on between family members, and how these communication patterns influenced individuals in the family. By consulting with whole families it was possible to experience the patterns of communication at first hand and to develop interventions. This created a shift from seeing symptoms as a reflection of the individual's internal conflict to understanding symptoms as providing a function within the family's dynamics. By creating changes in the family's communication patterns, changes at the individual level became possible.

The training in family therapy involves working with a team who are positioned behind a one-way mirror and the work is videoed. Before clients make appointments for therapy, the therapist needs to explain the process, as the clients have to give their consent. If clients really do not want to be videoed, then this view is respected. The idea is that two or more heads are better than one, and so the clients benefit from the resources of the whole team. At first, this seemed a daunting concept as a trainee therapist, but I quickly realized the advantages of being able to take occasional breaks to consult with the team and to use their suggestions to further the process. Sometimes, the therapist would feed back the team's ideas. At other times, the team would join with the clients and therapist, and tentatively reflect on what they had heard, making connections which would, ideally, be enriching and enhancing for the clients. The clients were told they could listen or not listen, so there was no onus on them to take the reflections on board. Afterwards, they were given the opportunity to comment, and often they said that this was the most valuable part of the therapy. Systemic/family therapists take the view that there is no one solution or one way forward, and, by creating several possible ideas, the clients may relate to one of them. When the team joins with the clients, this is one way to reduce the power differential between the team and the clients. At other times, the clients may watch the team discussions from behind the screen. However, once I qualified, it was impossible to have the luxury of a team, except when I worked as part of a family therapy team in a child and adolescent clinic. Working in private practice, I have to rely on supervision, or imagine what the team would be saying if they were present.

During my training in the early 1990s, my training organization became very interested in social constructionist ideas. The theory of social constructionism fits well with systemic ideas, since it takes the view that meanings emerge in conversations between people, rather than taking the more usual psychological perspective that people have attributes inherent within them. This view holds the notion that, throughout life, people are influenced by significant conversations, which can be verbal or non-verbal. Very often, these significant conversations take place in the family, but, equally, they can emanate from the field of education, religion, culture, society, media, etc. These conversations affect how people see themselves and how they create their identities. In turn, these identities, and their view of the world, affect how individuals relate to other people. At first, it was difficult to "unlearn" the psychological theories I had studied during my social work training, but, gradually, I began to see the benefits of focusing on the meanings, and how they had developed through language and communication. When social constructionism was incorporated in the training, we assumed the title of systemic/social constructionist therapists.

The training included a heuristic called the co-ordinated management of meaning (Pearce, 1976). This is a rather complicated title, but it does provide possible explanations as to how repetitive patterns are kept in place. This model describes how individuals can get trapped in cycles, or "strange loops", (Pearce, 1994, p. 64), and how various significant conversations or messages can have an impact on their relationships. Therefore, it assists in understanding the complexity of a client's narrative and dilemmas. A "strange loop" occurs when two competing stories or narratives create different behaviours, and these behaviours will oscillate, depending on which story or narrative is most prevalent at any one time.

For example, Figure 8 depicts a loop that I was tied into for many years.

This loop was held in place by my family story of "don't talk, just get on with life", and so my preferred way of being was just to get on with life, but sometimes this became too difficult, and so I would talk. However, there would come a point when this sense of being dependent seemed unnatural or strange, and I would flip back into my more usual way of operating in being independent and not talking. Moving to a different part of the loop did not create a long-term change. In my case, it was the family script or story that had to change, but for others it could be, for example, an educational, media, religious story, etc. Through my training as a systemic/social constructionist therapist, I began to see how this dualistic thinking is a very limited way of viewing the world. There are other possibilities and meanings. Holding on to the family script meant that I could not be independent and talk about problems or seek advice,

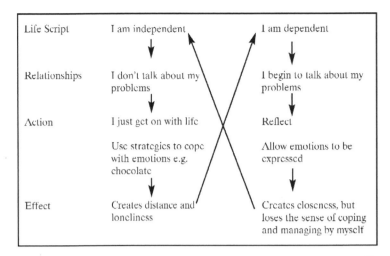

Life Script	I am independent	I am dependent
Relationships	I don't talk about my problems	I begin to talk about my problems
Action	I just get on with life	Reflect
	Use strategies to cope with emotions e.g. chocolate	Allow emotions to be expressed
Effect	Creates distance and loneliness	Creates closeness, but loses the sense of coping and managing by myself

Figure 8.

whereas it is perfectly possible to do both, and having a conversation permits different perspectives to emerge. Indeed, this is the whole purpose of therapy, from whatever modality.

If individuals develop identities that work well, then these patterns are not so evident, but for those of us who have developed a limiting self-story, these patterns become very obvious. Often, people can describe the patterns of their relationships, but they have no idea how they got into them, and less idea of how to get out of them. Sometimes strategies, like my own, are developed to overcome difficulties at a certain stage of life, and if these strategies are effective, they can become more generalized to deal with different situations throughout life. However, strategies that are developed for particular contexts frequently become outmoded in later circumstances. Hence, the work in systemic/social constructionist therapy is often to identify and highlight these ways of relating that are out of date, and to develop a repertoire of abilities, which can operate in different contexts.

Social constructionist therapy involves working collaboratively with clients to create new meanings. As therapists bring their own life experiences, identity stories, and ways of being to the dialogue, their personal and professional stories can be beneficial, or limiting, for example, provided the therapist has emerged from their dilemmas, this can sometimes bring hope in the midst of despair, and act as a resource. However, if the therapist joins with the client's account, because their own story is too close to what they are hearing, they can lose their curiosity, or choose not to explore a particular path, and this can be limiting. Self-reflexivity on the part of the therapist is essential to systemic/social constructionist therapy, and so I have to constantly monitor what effect my stories are having on the conversation. Curiosity, from this modality, is vital in helping clients reflect on the stories they are telling. By stepping outside the problem, or viewing it in a different way, it is possible to allow a different story to emerge. As with all therapeutic modalities, it is not possible to change life experiences, but the way you view them can change. From a systemic/social constructionist stance, we would make the distinction between the "stories lived" and the "stories told" (Pearce, 1994). Through this process it is possible to rewrite the life script in a way that is more empowering. Often, the details of how the client acted with agency are omitted from the narrative that is being told. By enriching the story told, and emphasizing these details, new identities and ways of being can emerge. In this way, systemic/social constructionist therapists are constantly searching for the nuggets and snippets in the storyline that will create a more empowering account. If I am to co-create a more enhancing story with a client, I need to constantly explore whether my own stories contribute to the empowerment or disempowerment of the client's story, even though I consider myself to be a liberal thinker.

When I work with couples, families, people in other relationships, or with individuals, it is important to validate each person's viewpoint and to accept differences of opinion. In this way I keep a neutral stance. That is not to say that everyone is equal. Issues of abuse are not condoned, but explored, to try to help the person abusing his or her power to understand the effects of their actions. One example of how this might be done is to interview them as if they were the victim, so they can step outside their own shoes and into another's. When children are in the room, it is important to amplify their voices and help them to express their views in a way they may never have done before. Often, behaviour is described as malicious, naughty, deliberate, etc., and by helping a child to describe their view of the situation, and what effect the communication is having on them, a previously untold story can unfold. The work is, then, to develop new patterns that can create different ways of relating. When important adults bear witness to children's stories, new dialogues can then evolve.

I will now give an account of a case study that will, I hope, illustrate these ideas. I worked with this man while I was training, and used some of the details in my MSc (Critchley, 2006), and so, in that context, I obtained informed consent for the information to be published. The name and some details have been changed to protect confidentiality.

Case study

Oscar was a white, thirty-eight-year-old man, who was sexually, physically, and emotionally abused by female members of his family and a male acquaintance from an extremely young age. Although Oscar's parents did not participate in the sexual abuse, Oscar never felt close to his mother, who frequently physically abused him, for example, locking him in a cupboard for long periods. Oscar's father was often absent, as he worked away from home, and when Oscar tried to tell his mother about the sexual abuse, she did not believe him. During Oscar's childhood he did not have a supportive adult, as the family lived quite an isolated existence. Like many children in his situation, Oscar closed the abuse off from his mind and did not begin to have flashbacks/memories of the abuse until he was thirty-five years old.

The flashbacks facilitated the reclaiming of his history, which he had shut away for so many years, and provided a possible explanation for his repetitive patterns of behaviour. Oscar felt that all the relationships in which he participated eventually became abusive. Although he made great efforts to foster relationships, he always became exhausted with his endeavours, and eventually the relationships would end. He was aware of being enmeshed in repetitive patterns, but he could not understand them.

Oscar lived a life of many ambiguities that he could not reconcile, and which left him feeling disconnected from others. In social situations, Oscar felt his voice was weakened, and that others knew the "rules" of life, but they remained a mystery to him. When Oscar was a child, the family rules were not clear, and they seemed to be made up on an *ad hoc* basis. What was interesting was that despite his experience, Oscar had a well developed sense of social responsibility, and showed considerable concern for others.

My life story does not parallel Oscar's in terms of the abuse that he suffered, but the experience of not being able to talk after my mother died does have similarities. The idea that nobody would understand what I was going through squashed my voice, and this created a distance, to some extent, with others. Also, my family had not been social beings, and I was often told not to talk about this and that outside the home. As I did not understand the reasons behind these injunctions, I would often just not talk, rather than risk making a mistake. So, this pattern of choosing not to talk outside the family had been established long before my mother's death, but afterwards it was not possible to talk about it, even inside the family. My family's pattern of communicating had contributed to one of my identities of being shy. I hoped that this sensitivity to Oscar's dilemma proved to be a resource rather than a limitation, as I struggled to enrich and empower his story.

One similarity I found between my own story-telling and that of Oscar's was that when your voice is squashed and you do not talk about your experiences, it is difficult to create a coherent storyline about your life. When the account of one's life experience is fragmented, it is through talking, writing, drawing, or play (in the case of children) that the descriptions become enriched. My therapy involved writing about my recollections, and this seemed to be an easier medium for me to communicate my thoughts. Oscar, on the other hand, seemed to value the opportunity to talk, and used the oral tradition to make sense of his life. Through the talking, he gradually came to provide a more articulate explanation of his life.

However, whereas I was just unclear about what could be said or not said outside the family, in other areas of family life the rules of what was permitted or not permitted were understandable. On the other hand, none of the family rules was clear for Oscar. When Oscar tried to tell his mother about the abuse, he was not believed. As with many children who are abused and have no one to turn to who will believe them, they often deny their own accounts, and accept the adult's views regarding the experience, for example, "you have had a dream". The family had socially constructed a story that the abuse had not happened, and so Oscar came to believe that no one would believe him. If he tried to tell someone he would be seen as a liar, and so it was easier to deny his own experience and put it out of his mind. In mental health language, this is seen as dissociation.

Oscar was an extremely religious person, and it was these strong beliefs that helped him through his darkest days. In the context of him being a religious person, he saw himself as a truthful person. However, the idea that he would be seen as a liar if he talked about the abuse had an effect on the therapy, because how did he know I would believe him. Oscar used the metaphor of a maze to describe his dilemma . . . *it feels like I'm stuck in the middle of a maze and it is easy if you have a map, and if you haven't you're stuck*. Here, Oscar describes his feeling of paralysis, as he does not know how to go on. The family story had the effect of positioning Oscar as a liar if he hung on to his story, and as confused if he chose the family story, which discounted his own story.

My training as a systemic/social constructionist therapist had taught me that it was not essential for clients to talk about the details of their abuse if they did not want to, and it was possible to work with the effects of the abuse. In the earlier sessions of working with Oscar, I was very concerned about his fragility, and I was afraid that he might become suicidal if he connected too closely with his trauma. Oscar had assured me that his religious beliefs prevented him from suicidal acts, as he was fearful of the consequences when he eventually met with God in the afterlife. At a later date, I worked with Oscar regarding his relationship with God, as his ideas about God appeared to be very punitive. At this point, however, the information did not totally assuage my fears for him.

I decided to express my dilemma quite transparently, and the transcript is as follows:

SL   Maybe you need to think before you leap. I have some sense of you standing on the edge wanting to tell a story, but don't want to tell the story. What effect would it have to tell the story at this point?

O   I think the absolute truth and fear is that you won't believe me and that you will think that I'm making it up and that you'll say I'm wasting your time and you will tell me to go. That's my honest opinion.

This had not been the reply I had been expecting, but, nevertheless, it provided some very useful information, and helped me to understand the dilemma that Oscar faced. Given that therapy is a context in which concerns are discussed, it would seem that if Oscar talked in the way he wanted, he thought he would not be believed and that the therapy would end. On the other hand, if he did not talk he would be wasting my time, and the result would be the same, in that the therapy would end. I reassured Oscar that I would believe him and that the therapy would continue.

Oscar did begin to talk about the abuse, and this helped him to understand some of the patterns in which he was trapped, and how these patterns affected his life.

During the telling of the story, Oscar had an overwhelming desire to reassure me. While being abused, Oscar had to tell his abusers how nice they were, and this response had become an automatic reaction in relationships. In taking the position of a caring person, Oscar tended to look after others in relationships, but this became exhausting, and he would then feel that the only solution would be to end the relationship. Oscar had never learnt how to ask for help, or get his own needs met. In fact, it was his brother who sought therapy for him. In relationships, Oscar acted as if he could cope, while all the time feeling very insecure. He would become angry that the care he showed never seemed to be reciprocated, but he never understood how he contributed to this pattern.

At this point, I was reminded that when I was a child and I was asked about my mother, I would reply that she was dead, and then people would often get very embarrassed and flustered. I, in turn, felt that I had to comfort them and say it was all right, and any feelings I had about mentioning the death of my mother had to become secondary. My experiences of reassuring others are quite different from Oscar's, but it was a resource to remind me to keep focused on Oscar's needs, and to reassure him when appropriate, or to provide some possible explanations to help the process.

As Oscar became older, he sometimes refused to comply with the abuse, as he had done when he was younger, but when he did this he inevitably felt very guilty. This guilt had the effect of preventing Oscar from caring for himself and attending to his own needs. To do so would be seen as selfish. These moments of refusal could have pointed towards Oscar developing agency for himself, but this richer story had never been considered before. Although Oscar knew the abuse was wrong, and that the adults in his life were not good care-givers, he had never made the connection with how the abuse affected the patterns of relationships in the present.

My experience of growing up was almost the opposite of Oscar's, in terms of assuming responsibility. I was born when my parents were middle-aged, and my upbringing was a very protected one. Oscar, on the other hand, grew up without the normal nurturing that a child should expect, and, indeed, he had to assume the responsibility of meeting the needs of adults. When I reflected upon this idea with Oscar, it did help to assuage some of his guilt, as he had never thought in these terms before. Instead, he had always seen himself as selfish if he paid attention to his own needs, or refused to comply with the abuse even when he knew it was wrong.

Oscar's metaphor of *"it feels like I'm stuck in the middle of a maze and it is easy if you have a map, and if you haven't you're stuck"* seems to provide an apt description of how he related to life. Having tried many times to find a way out of the maze, Oscar had almost given up trying, as he always ended up in the same repetitive pattern.

Using the heuristic provided by CMM (Pearce, 1976), several explanations as to how these repetitive patterns are kept in place emerge. A number of stories appeared to influence each other, and compound Oscar's dilemma when talking about the sexual abuse.

The relationships between the "stories lived and told" (Pearce, 1994), in the context of Oscar telling his story of sexual abuse in childhood, are as follows:

Therapeutic cultural stories	In therapy you talk about your problems
Family myth	Oscar imagines things
Relationship stories	Oscar looks after others
Life script	I am a liar
Episode/context	The dilemma when talking about experiences of sexual abuse

In my case, it was the family story of "don't talk just get on with life" which kept the repetitive pattern in place, but Oscar's many-layered stories were interwoven into complex patterns, which were all interrelated.

One loop which helps to explain Oscar's dilemma in talking about the sexual abuse in therapy is depicted in Figure 9.

In the context of having a self concept of being a liar when talking about the abuse, which is informed by the family myth, Oscar felt he would not be believed, but in the context of not talking about the abuse, he thought he would not be able to justify his presence in therapy, and he would be wasting my time. Oscar's intransigent pattern trapped him in an impossible position within the therapeutic relationship. However, as Oscar did talk about the abuse, the effect of the story "I am a liar and will not be believed" must have weakened.

Another repetitive pattern that emerged was that, as Oscar was coming to therapy, he was presumably hoping for some help, but whenever he tried to care for himself he felt guilty and started to reassure others, which reduced the feelings of guilt, but left him feeling exhausted (Figure 10).

Again this pattern, which had a detrimental effect on Oscar's relationships, could have had the same effect on our relationship, and the result could have been similar, in that the relationship would have ended prematurely.

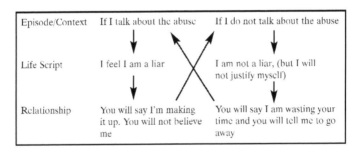

Figure 9.

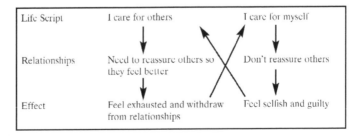

Figure 10.

From a social constructionist point of view, my stories have an impact on the meanings that emerge within the therapeutic conversation, and so I considered what they might be.

My professional stories are as shown in Figure 11.

This, however, is not a "strange loop", as, although I could oscillate between the two positions, I was not trapped in the cycle. I could make choices and judgements as to which response to give, depending on whether Oscar decided to talk about the abuse or not.

As Oscar did tell his story of abuse, and he did remain in therapy with me for many years, my stories must have helped to reduce the influence of his powerful stories, and weaken the strength of his patterns. Oscar's mental health improved, and he gained in confidence to come into the world again. He reconnected with old friendships and made new ones. He continues to have ups and downs, and occasionally comes back for a few sessions, but, on the whole, he is managing his life.

Systemic/social constructionist therapy does not work with transference, but all ideas are useful, and sometimes I do consider how I am feeling, and use that as information to be explored. No psychotherapy emerges in isolation, and family therapy evolved out of psychodynamic therapy, and so, inevitably, it has its influences. However, the main focus of systemic/social constructionist therapy is to be reflexive to how my stories influence and affect the client's stories, and, conversely, how the client's stories affect my stories, and so this examination goes around in a recursive loop.

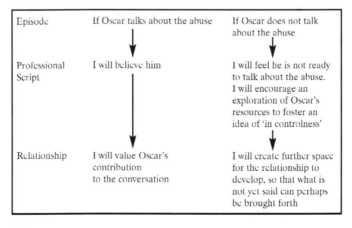

Episode	If Oscar talks about the abuse	If Oscar does not talk about the abuse
Professional Script	I will believe him	I will feel he is not ready to talk about the abuse. I will encourage an exploration of Oscar's resources to foster an idea of 'in controlness'
Relationship	I will value Oscar's contribution to the conversation	I will create further space for the relationship to develop, so that what is not yet said can perhaps be brought forth

Figure 11.

As this therapy involves creating new meanings, which affect behaviour and relationship patterns, it also has similarities to cognitive–behavioural therapy. Within the systemic/social constructionist community, the ideas are constantly developing, and so the therapy remains challenging and interesting and offers possibilities to explore relationships directly with all those involved.

Your reflection

- Consider a conversation that you have had with a friend or a client, when what you said had an impact on the other's worldview and, in turn, your views also changed, so that a new meaning emerged for both of you during the dialogue.

Further reading

McNamee, S., & Gergen, K. J. (Eds) (1992). *Therapy as a Social Construction*. London: Sage.

I have chosen this book as it had a great influence on me when I was training, and helped me to understand how the concepts of social constructionism can be put into practice in therapy. It contains a series of papers by authors who practise in different ways within a systemic framework, and so there are many examples and case studies demonstrating how reflexivity is used.

CHAPTER SIX

Francesca's story: working with the givens of life

I have been working as a counsellor in agencies, schools, and in private practice for some ten years. My focus has been on relationships: I have worked with couples at Relate and with teenagers in school. I have recently become involved in setting up the first counselling service offered specifically for people born with defects caused by Thalidomide.

I am interested in working with the "givens" of life, as the existentialists call it. There is an inevitable aspect to life for us all. There are things that we cannot easily change or make go away.

Working existentially means different things for different people. To me, it involves staying with what Heidegger called the *Dasein*. This is about both acceptance of who we are and taking responsibility for what we can be within the framework of givens. There is the *sein*-side to life, which involves defining ourselves in relation to others. This involves taking charge of our being-in-the-world, with authenticity in mind. Van Deurzen (2002) writes:

> Authentic living is about being able to make clear and well-informed choices in accordance with the values one recognizes as worth committing oneself to ... not drifting along with what is "done" and not "done". [p. 48]

I was born a Thalidomide victim, and have an upper arm disability. I never felt I had issues about having a disability, but, as I got older, I began to realize I was feeling extremely angry. I decided to enter into personal therapy, which I had for five years. Finally, I was able to let go of my anger and feelings of loss without feeling guilty. The guilt, I began to realize, was about my relationship with my parents: the guilt my parents felt because of my mother taking the drug Thalidomide, and the guilt I felt for seeing their sad faces at times. My personal therapy was a life-changing experience, and I feel it offered me another way of living my life. I began to realize that life was choiceful, despite the givens of being born different.

Meeting Janet

It was a Monday morning when I received a phone call from Janet asking to see me concerning her issues around her disability. She sounded softly spoken, and I could sense a feeling of immense sadness. I arranged that I would see her the next day at 11 a.m. for an assessment session. I felt slightly nervous about seeing Janet, as she, too, was a victim of Thalidomide and had an upper arm disability. I wondered how seeing someone similar to me would make me feel, and what impact this would have on our counselling relationship.

The doorbell went at 11 a.m., and as I walked to open the door I felt my heartbeat quickening. Opening the door, I was met by a tall, slightly overweight blonde lady wearing glasses. We shook hands, and Janet walked into the counselling room. The session opened with Janet talking about the anger she was feeling, and this was affecting her marriage. Janet saw this as the issue she wanted to have help in exploring with me. As the session unfolded, I noticed that my heartbeat had calmed down and I was feeling extremely warm towards Janet. I was finding her conversation entertaining and I noticed that despite Janet looking timid, she was very chatty and warm with an open smile.

Janet's disability was similar to mine, and, after a short time into the session, I realized that I had forgotten about Janet's disability. People had often said to me, "You don't even notice your arms after meeting you". I found this comment hard to believe or understand, as, for me, the first I see of myself when I look into a mirror is my arms. Yet, here I was counselling a lady and realizing that I had forgotten about her arms! The assessment session was drawing to an end, and Janet and I decided that we would meet once a week and begin to explore her anger. After she left, I began to reflect on our first meeting.

Neither I nor Janet had made any comment about our disabilities. Was there any meaning to be made here? When would I start to explore her meaning around her disability, and how would I feel listening to this? We would have different experiences, and how would this make me feel? Would I self-disclose about my experiences, and, if I did, would this be helpful to her or would it be about my need? Had she ever talked deeply about being born disabled? Looking at all these unanswered questions, I was aware that I would need close supervision and to give myself a longer reflection time after seeing Janet. I was aware of the importance of staying with Janet and her experience, in the way that I think van Deurzen (2002) captures well.

The existential counsellor or therapist needs to come to the sessions with complete openness to the individual situation and with an attitude of wonder that will allow the specific circumstances and experiences to unfold in their own right. Assisting other human beings in understanding their own life in a genuine and meaningful manner is a serious matter. Each and every discovery is personal and unpredictable. *We can however distinguish a number of themes that will often emerge in this process.* [*ibid.*]

How could I link myself to Janet without putting my own battle with authenticity upon her?

As I sat down with my supervisor and I began to talk about meeting Janet, I felt my heart racing and my mouth became dry. My supervisor noticed with me that I was sounding anxious. We stopped talking about Janet, and talked about what I was feeling right now. I spoke about how strange I felt seeing someone else being affected by the drug Thalidomide. I had never met anyone before who was a victim of Thalidomide, and I began to realize since seeing Janet that I had been also denying my physical disability for the majority of my life, trying to fit in, and fighting to prove myself. Meeting Janet had shown me that she, too, had been living this way, and had become exhausted with having to fight, and was now feeling angry. This was how I had been feeling before I had entered into personal therapy. Talking this through with my supervisor, it became clear that I needed to watch very closely not to over-identify with Janet, and to be alert for any parallel processes. I may have a strong desire to "rescue" Janet by telling her what to do from my experience. It was imperative for me to stay with her "phenomenology", in the way Yalom writes about: "The . . . existential analyst must approach the patient's phenomenology; that is, he or she must enter the patient's experiential world" (1980, p. 17).

I felt less anxious meeting Janet for the second session. I felt more grounded with my feelings and felt able to put them aside as we both sat down for the session. Janet started by saying how angry she had been since our last session, and it had been particularly bad the other morning when she was trying to do what she felt was a simple task of drying her hair. She could not manage to hold her hairbrush and blow-wave her hair with the hairdryer. Janet had learnt to manage this task for many years, but, over the past six months, she had been getting a lot of arthritic pain in her finger joints. This, she knew, was because of her disability, and she began to feel frightened about her future. This fear she felt this particular morning, and began to shout and scream at her husband. Janet said, looking back, she realized how irrational she was being, but, at the time, she could not stop herself. As she was becoming engrossed in telling me this story, I began to feel my heart racing, my mouth becoming dry, and my hands were sweating. I felt incredibly tearful, and I could feel tears welling up in my eyes. I tried very hard to keep grounded and to be available to Janet. I chose not to share how I was feeling with Janet and decided to stay detached, and we agreed to meet next week.

After she left, I began to write some session notes and began crying while writing Janet's story about drying her hair. I started to remember a particular incident when I was fourteen and I was drying my hair. I could not get the style quite right. My mother came and offered help, and I started to shout at her and I, too, became irrational. I realized as I was writing that the main theme was around "vulnerability". Janet was frightened about her future, at having to rely on others to help her. This was something that I had picked up on so strongly because it resonated with me. The memory from when I was fourteen was about fear and about having to rely on my mother to help me. But, at fourteen, I had enough "fight" in me to prove to the world that I could dry my hair! Perhaps Janet was talking about being tired of fighting? Perhaps the important thing was to stay with the feeling?

I began to think about why Janet had come to counselling in the first place. Maybe she was trying to say that she was tired, at the age of forty-seven, of having to keep on fighting to prove herself. But words failed her; she sounded cheerful and happy; she made me laugh. I began to focus on trying to listen to what she told me underneath. She was now at a stage in her life at which, deep down, she needed to face her disability and her feelings of having to rely on others. Her mind and body were getting physically tired. Viewed from this angle, I wondered if I had carried her vulnerability in our session.

I felt much better having reflected on this session, and I was looking forward to seeing Janet. On the day she was due, I decided to wear a new skirt and shirt I had bought. I felt very professional looking in the mirror, and I felt very much in control. I sat and waited for Janet to arrive. Fifteen minutes later, Janet still had not arrived, and I began to feel agitated. As the time drew to the close of what should have been a session with Janet, I began to panic. What had happened to her? Had I done something wrong? I hoped she was all right. I was relieved that I was having supervision that afternoon, and would be able to share my concerns.

I shared with my supervisor what I had reflected on after the session concerning Janet's anger at not being able to dry her own hair. My supervisor asked me how I was feeling about my future. Did I have any pains? Was I worried about having to rely on others? I began to realize that I was also really frightened and feeling vulnerable. It was not just Janet's fear of vulnerability that had been around in the session, it was also my own despair and exhaustion. We looked at the next session and how to handle it. If Janet was going to come back, I needed to be authentic. Right now, this meant being more honest, open, and real with her. I needed to self-disclose about my feelings after the last session. The fact that I, too, was a victim of Thalidomide was obvious for us both. There was neither reason nor possibility for me to pretend that I did not share some of Janet's experiences. Talking it through with my supervisor, we both came to realize that I had been too detached in the sessions. This was partly because of protecting me, but also because of trying to assess whether self-disclosing would be appropriate.

The time came for Janet to arrive, and I was feeling anxious as to whether she would come this week. The doorbell did ring, and, as I opened the door, Janet gave her warm smile, and we walked into the counselling room. Janet said she had felt angry with me after the last session; she felt that I had not understood about her anger with not being able to dry her hair. I felt myself taking a big breath, and I opened up to her about how I had been feeling listening to her story. I described a similar incident when I was much younger, and how it had made me feel vulnerable, and how difficult it was for me to accept this feeling. As I was self-disclosing, I began to notice Janet's eyes widening, her legs uncrossing, and she leant forward, earnestly listening. When I stopped, she looked at me and said, "Thank you so much for sharing this with me. I can't tell you how much it helps to hear someone else feeling like I did. Listening to you I can now see that when I shouted at my husband I had tears rolling down my face. I felt so confused by this." She then began to talk about how difficult it was as a child to cry. Her mother would cry a lot of the time. Her father was rarely at home. She felt she could not share any sad feelings with her mother because she did not want her to cry. I could sense that Janet and I had entered into a real relationship. An adult-to-adult relationship, or what Buber would call an I–Thou experience, where we really met through a shared experience. I was not pretending to be a detached professional counsellor. I was being open and real with my client; a person, a fellow human being, who could cope with seeing life from the angle that Janet experienced life from sometimes.

Reflecting on this session afterwards, I realized that self-disclosing with this particular client was really useful. We had entered into a real relationship where I was open and honest, which enabled Janet to feel she, too, could be the same. I felt she now could share whatever feelings she wanted to and she could trust that I could hold / contain her feelings without judgement. But I was also aware that self-disclosing does not suit every client. It is imperative to share openly and honestly your feelings about clients with your supervisor, and to reflect what the client might gain from my self-disclosing. I also reflected on my personal therapy and how useful this had been for me. I had worked through my anger over the years, and I am able to reflect now the feelings I am covering with my anger. For me, personally, anger can cover two main themes: vulnerability and shame. These two themes have been "givens", being born different in this society.

Reflections on being born a victim of Thalidomide using existential theory

I mentioned the existentialism term "givens" in the beginning of this text. I would like to return to this with my own experiences in mind.

Existential theory states that humans have four ultimate dilemmas to face in their lives: death, freedom, isolation, and meaninglessness. "The individual's confrontation with each of these facts of life constitutes the content of the existential dynamic conflict" (Yalom, 1980, p. 8).

Relating this theory to me, I see that my main dilemma throughout my life has been to deal with fear of isolation and meaninglessness. I would like to look at these two dilemmas separately.

Isolation

Humans are relationship-seeking creatures. As humans, we need to feel that we belong, to feel accepted by others. I see our first experiences of belonging as in our family of origin. From a very young age, I always had a feeling of being different within my family. Only with entering into the therapy world did I start to reflect on this feeling, and I began to see that I looked physically different, and my character was very loud and confident. This was different from the rest of my family. My loud and confident manner continued through my school life and beyond. These ways of being made me get noticed—not for my arms, but for my "out there" personality! This was my personal "fight" to feel accepted and to belong in my family and society. My family, because they would feel relieved of the "guilt" of Thalidomide, and they could see that I was happy and had friends. Society could see that I was "OK" and maybe had something to offer.

At this point, I would like to look at intrapersonal isolation. This is where a person partitions parts of themselves. I never saw myself as disabled. I would never look at my arms in the mirror. In other words, I chose to see what I wanted. I never wanted to meet other Thalidomide victims. When I saw items in the newspapers, I would never think of myself as like them. I lived in a world with able-bodied people, and, as far as I was concerned, this was where I belonged. As I began to grow older, I started to notice people's stares. Their tone of voice would sometimes sound patronizing, or people would avoid me. Some people would question why I looked the way I did. All of these experiences were shocking to me. I could not understand why people could not see me as "normal". The biggest shock for me came when I was in my mid thirties and, as a family, we applied to immigrate to Australia. I had to be seen by a consultant orthopaedic surgeon, who had to write to the Australian Immigration authorities to say I would be an asset to their country. Unfortunately, Australia did not agree, and refused a visa on the grounds of my disability. When I learnt of this news my world came to a dramatic halt. This felt like an ultimate rejection of me as a person. A country had made a decision that I did not belong there. Everything I had believed in about myself was thrown into doubt. It was at this point that I entered therapy, and began to realize that I had spent years denying that I had a physical disability. This had been my defence mechanism, which had proved to be useful for some of my life, but I needed now to stop isolating this part of myself and look at how I could begin to learn to intergrate my arms and my feelings of my physical self.

Meaninglessness

What meaning does life have? Why do we live? How shall we live? These questions can occur at different times of our lives, often happening at times when we may be in some heightened state of distress/anxiety.

I was brought up as a Catholic, and the meaning I made early on in my life as to why I was born a victim of Thalidomide was because I had done something wrong. God was punishing me. As I write this sentence, I think about how frightening this meaning must have been for me as a little girl. As I grew up, I often thought, what have I done wrong? I decided very early on I needed to be a good girl, and be this so called "perfect" friend, wife, and mother. I always had to get it right. When I got it wrong, I went to an extreme place of shame. The feeling of shame could last for weeks. Sometimes, I could reach a place where I would ask, "why am I here"? At this awful low place I would imagine taking my own life, but somehow I managed to find the energy to pull myself out of the pit of shame.

Entering into personal therapy I began to see I could create another meaning for my life. A meaning less punishing, with no punishing God. The journey of creating another meaning for why I exist has been hard and long. I have turned my back on the Catholic faith, and have embraced God as a kind energy who does not belong to rules of how to behave. I believe that God is around me and has many plans for me, and that I am an "OK" person to exist in this world. When I get it wrong, I do not go to a place of shame. I am able to accept that I am not "perfect" and it is all right to make a mistake. There are times that I can revert back to the old meaning of feeling punished, but these times are far fewer.

A personal note

Writing this chapter has been very challenging. I have put off writing it so many times, often due to negative thoughts. The main thought was, "I am not good enough to do this". Being asked to write and to be part of a wonderful writing group did not match the meaning society put on me being a victim of Thalidomide. According to the medical world, when I was born I was not meant to grow; my brain, they felt, would be affected. The school I went to did not think I would be able to cope with academia. The meanings I had made, about which I spoke earlier, confirmed these statements.

At the moment, I am involved in a pilot study counselling other Thalidomide people over the phone. The main theme for them has been that they have always had to fight their way through the judgements society has made about them. I share this feeling with the people I have counselled. There are some of them who are angry about having to fight, and there are some who are tired of fighting. I feel less angry, and I do not feel I now have to prove anything to anyone else. This chapter has been a personal challenge. I feel empowered in that I have challenged the meanings I and others have made. I also feel that I belong in the world I exist in.

Your reflection

● Please consider a "given" in your own life, for example, an illness, bereavement, a lack of meaning or direction. How did you did you deal with these issues for yourself and with your clients?

Recommended reading

Yalom, I. (1999). *Momma and the Meaning of Life: Tales of Psychotherapy.* New York: Piatkus Books.

The reason I chose this book is that it gave me permission for being "human". I was struggling during my Relate training with the feeling of not being a good enough counsellor. I felt I was not getting it "right" for my clients. Through reading this book, I discovered that it was not about getting it "right", it was about learning about myself through the relationship with my clients. Irvin Yalom's honesty in his writing about what he learnt about himself and his clients through their relationship is profound. Reading this book, I began to understand that I needed to go to a deeper level, both personally and professionally. Through this realization I chose to enter personal therapy and to undertake a diploma in counselling.

CHAPTER SEVEN

Sherna's story: cults, culture, and context

*T*he supervision group was tense. The three trainee psychotherapists sat in a circle slightly closer to each other, with the supervisor making the fourth. This was the time when they presented their case studies, and one of their number was presenting her case. They looked like the usual group. One was clearly from another culture, with her dark skin and black hair. She was presenting her case of providing therapy to a client from her own culture. The tension in the group increased as the case was presented and the supervisor spoke. ". . . the point is that you are not being congruent here. Your response is not real. During this session I sense that something is not in synch. You are not being real." The trainee looked despairing. "What can I say or do to make myself seem real to you?"

I am a psychoanalytic psychotherapist who has trained in intercultural therapy. I was born in Bombay, India, and came to the UK in 1978. I trained in integrative counselling, and then went on to do a Masters in Psychoanalytic Intercultural Psychotherapy. I was born into a Parsee family. Parsees are a minority community who follow an ancient religion called Zoroastrianism, which originated in Persia. I was brought up, in an atmosphere flushed with the excitement of winning Indian independence, in novel and enlightened ways. The Indian freedom struggle was quintessentially an Indian experiment carved from Indian philosophy and practice involving discipline, self-denial, and patience. Along with millions of Indians, my parents had been involved in the freedom struggle. When I look back, I see my childhood as one fused with the fortunes of India. A whole generation of Indians share this common bond. It was an exciting time to be alive. A combination of politics and philosophy pervaded our thinking. There was a firm belief in equality, in breaking down divisions, shaking traditions and shifting old prejudices.

I was brought up in a family where my grandfather was the authority. He was strict but fair, and a little remote. It was said in the family that I had the ability to melt his hard heart. Being the youngest of the family (my sister and the cousins), I was cosseted and indulged. During my childhood, I encountered the usual variety of illnesses, chicken pox and measles. So did my elder sister, but she always had a more virulent form of illness. And once I remember her lying in bed surrounded by my anxious mother and an aunt. I had just had the measles, and it had not had that effect on me. I felt guilty that she was more ill with the same disease.

My mother was a clever, broadminded woman. Her own father had died when she was young, and she, being the eldest of two daughters, had to start work early in her life. She trained as a teacher, but she gave that up when she married. Our family was often getting together and visiting each other. There was an aunt of my father's who was a great storyteller. She had remained single and had often helped in looking after all the children in the family. We all knew that my sister was her favourite. She told the most wonderful stories, and sitting around her in the darkening evening she would tell us in serial form the stories from the Mahabharata and Ramayana. All the characters came to life and became part of my imagination. Heroic warriors, family sagas, envious stepmothers, virtuous women, family honour, armies massing, battles between good and bad. Contained within the Mahabharata's elaborate cast and stories is the

> philosophical base which provides its members with a sanctioned pattern, a template which can be superimposed on the outer world with all its uncertainties and on the flow of inner experience in all

its turbulence, thus helping individuals to make sense of their own lives. [Kakar, 1978]

Although we were told that this aunt was an angelic person, and clearly all the children adored her, this was not the view among the elders. There was some discussion describing her as interfering and meddlesome. The Mahabharata was spilling over into our family! I, too, felt a quickly submerged annoyance at her for loving my sister more than me and making no secret of it either!

My sister was a very good student in school. She came top of her class, was good at sport, and was generally considered a promising student. I was whimsical, not consistent in my school results, prone to temper, and in a constant battle of wills with my mother. My father was often away from home, and I fantasized that he would come and change everything. Again, the family script was that I was his favourite. My mother was often unhappy, inconsistent, and bowed down with family intrigues. In spite of her own unhappiness, she did offer much affirmation to both my sister and I, but we were drawn into the battles she had with family members and our father.

On a summer day in April 1964, the heat lay shimmering over the school playgrounds. The badminton and basketball courts were dried solid and dusty with the tramping of hundreds of girls to and from classes. Our convent school always had an assembly, with the headmistress dealing with the issues of the day, prayers, and, finally, a march leading us out and into our classrooms for the day. The nuns believed that marches would put us in the correct frame of mind for studies. I was fourteen years old, and, as usual, slightly bored, lounging with my friends in the back row of my class. But, on this day, the assembly was longer and we had a group visiting consisting of Rajmohan Gandhi, grandson of Mahatma Gandhi, accompanied by a cast from a musical called *Space is so Startling!* The cast, mainly made up of American and English members, entertained us with songs and speeches. I was riveted.

The message they brought was simple. It promised that the world could be changed by individual change. The message was so simple, the appeal so direct. The world had seen two world wars, hunger was everywhere, poverty stalked the land, brother fought with brother, and people yearned for a change. The change could begin from within with personal decisions and spread to make India a clean, strong, and united country. Absolute moral standards and God's guidance were the inner fuel for this revolution. It was not an organization that you could join, just something that you could live. And it claimed that it was not a religion, but an ideology.

This was my introduction to Moral Rearmament, which had been formed in response to the military armament taking place in Europe between the two world wars. The founder was an American Lutheran minister called Frank Buchman, and his baton had been taken up by various leaders from England. In India, it was led by Rajmohan Gandhi, tall, elegant, and very persuasive, a man of impeccable lineage, being not only the grandson of Mahatma Gandhi, but also of Rajagopalachari, India's first Governor General.

Hundreds responded and joined him from all over India. Even today, I meet people who were students in the early 1960s and who were attracted by this message. I was certainly hooked. Both my parents had been in the freedom struggle. I wanted to be part of the excitement of that time, too.

It was impossible to grow up in Bombay and be impervious to the conditions of others. Living in a crowded and cosmopolitan city, my family were comfortable, but we were never far from poverty and its effects in alcoholism, domestic violence, or endless anxiety and poor health, among others. When people came seeking help from my grandfather, I could relate to their despair. Why did I despair when I had all my family around me and never had a day without food or a roof over my head?

But somewhere in my relationship with my mother and our constant battles I had experience of what it felt like never to have any control over my life. Looking back, it would be crass to compare degrading poverty to my own situation. But the emotions I experienced gave me an insight into what it must be like to suffer.

I decided to jettison school and join Moral Rearmament. I gained my father's reluctant support, and spent the next seven years within this group, travelling, constantly spreading the message within India and abroad. My mother did not speak with me for almost a year after I had joined. Having gained a degree of independence, I feared that I had broken her heart. I wrote to her every day to keep her aware of what I was doing, and hoped that on some level she was not lost to me and would even be proud of me.

Slowly, she did thaw, and after a while began to take an interest in what I was doing.

I stayed with MRA for seven years, during which I formed some of the closest relationships of my life. My sister followed me into it and it provided us both with a very large community from around the globe. But, eventually, it was my ego's adaptive functions that enabled me to leave. I realized around a year before leaving that I simply did not believe in it any more. I was troubled by all the things that MRA claimed it was not. And I recognized that it was, in fact, a cult. A moderate cult, but with a cult's in-built structure.

I realized that I had ceased to believe in its central precepts. I had never been able to square with what the cult claimed it was and what it was in reality.

In common with other cults, MRA personified certain traits. These were:

- a simple message easily understood and containing mass appeal;
- a doctrine that touched on personal sadness;
- a promise that had a universal feel. A connection with the rest of the world;
- a sense of chosenness. This justified the sense of martyrdom. The feeling that we had to do the dirty work for the rest of society. Following from this was the demonizing of all critics and criticism;
- a single "Road to Damascus" conversion when miracles occurred, lives changed, and "God took over";
- the doctrinal ideology was accepted as self-evident, requiring no explanation or proof;
- MRA pursued and depended on the support of the great and the good for legitimacy. In the cultivation of this, the leaders justified a lifestyle far in excess to that of the ordinary people who worked within it;
- sameness was demanded and coerced, contradicting the common childhood experiences within the Indian context where differentness was natural;
- MRA was distinguished not by what it claimed to be, but the things it denied it was. Thus, it claimed not to be a Christian organization or an organization at all, simply calling itself an

ideology. Years later, I was to discover that the spread of Christianity was its central precept in its formation in the UK;

- powerful unspoken, unwritten rules and the use of peer pressure and authority, along with a stringent hierarchy, kept the organization running smoothly;
- an over-developed sense of guilt, through which control and dependency were ensured;
- a rigid and excessive work regime;
- dependency on the community, which replaced the family. The fact that my friendships remain to this day is a non-traumatic emotional debt to MRA.

The encounter with MRA was also my first experience of the West. Back in 1964, these were the first Westerners I had encountered. Over the next seven years, while the cultural interactions inevitably polluted and enriched, weakened and strengthened, blinded and enlightened, I began to believe that this encounter between a Christian group and Indian values was unequal and reductionist. The experience of colonialism and its in-built ideology of superiority and mastery over subject races left a legacy that could not be erased.

The lives of Indians have been touched by independence and the subsequent attempt to bring a national identity to bear. There has been much debate about the affect of Westernization and modernization. While the gaining of independence was the cumulative result of a mass movement involving sacrifice and suffering, this debate, when simplified, is represented by Gandhi and Nehru, the one favouring rural development, land reforms, continued revival of village crafts, and political decentralization, and the other stressing the need for industrialization, centralization, and modern science and technology. The social realignment that followed opting for the Nehru model has seen an enormous growth of a politically and economically powerful middle class. A whole generation of Indians has fused picaresque personal adventure and trajectories with the journey of the nation. We have made, according to our own ideas, what being an Indian means. Some are traditional, others are more stridently modern or Western. All eye the possibilities posed by the West. Nehru's vision of a modern India has developed in an ironic, deviant relationship to Western modernity, which inspired it.

The MRA notion of a single unit of the individual being able to galvanize and change society was a powerful message to post-independence Indians. Our parents had participated in a unique experiment and been successful, and perhaps this was our generation's chance for a similar experience. This depiction, springing from the worldview of individualistic change, diminishes our parents' collective, awe-inspiring achievement, for the freedom struggle was marked by a mass movement of a kind that merged our individualistic differences, Hindu, Muslim, male, female, rich, and poor.

The diminishing extended further. We talked a lot about India, but there was very little India within. Certainly no Indian music or literature. Perhaps the dining room arrangements illustrate the cultural impositions most precisely. An enormous amount of repetitive effort was centred around mealtimes, with high tables, table setting serving etiquette, and table manners. All of these were based on Western norms, with the implication that this was the best way to do things. This assumption pervaded all our waking hours.

Money was coerced, sexual activity of any kind was frowned upon, and power was maintained by way of early morning meetings where your attendance was mandatory. Denial being central to its functioning, we were always assured that this was an exercise in free will and nothing was compulsory. But the emotional pressure was great on anyone sleeping late, or seeking to do things other than those assigned to one. So many people went on to have nervous breakdowns, broken by the punishing work and the emotional pressure. Any minor error was treated as a moral shortcoming. The leaders who came from other parts of the world often suffered from fragile health. In the case of one of them, he would insist on having afternoon naps, which terrorized the entire house into silence in the middle of the day. Fragile health was another way of claiming martyrdom. So different from that other role model, Mahatma Gandhi, whose fasting and praying had galvanized the entire nation. In looking back, I now understand that my expectations of leaders had come from what I had learnt about the men who fought for Indian independence. And in this lay the basis of projection to the grandson of the Mahatma; my expectations built on the reputation of his grandfather.

By its very name, MRA was part of a European identity. It was born as The Oxford Group, and changed its name to Moral

Rearmament as a response to the military rearmament that accompanied the Second World War. Since then, it has changed its name at least twice. The search for its identity, thus exemplified in the name changes and its inner conflict, remains unresolved. MRA's appeal lay in a set of ideas, which were based on mundane, evangelizing, social influence.

A crucial moment came when, at the age of twenty-one and newly returned to India after travelling continuously for seven years, I decided that I had to leave MRA. This remains the single most premeditated and considered act of my life—the ego's adaptive function. I was the first from among my close friends who had joined MRA in 1964 who decided to leave. In the six months that it took to make the decision, a central reason was the sense that, by staying within the MRA community, I was postponing the decision to join the world of grown-ups. This was a time of coming together, a settling of peace. I realized that I did not share the worldview of human nature as being deviant and sinful and only redeemable by God's intervention. I discovered later, when I studied world religions, that this is a Christian belief not shared by Hinduism or my own religion. And there I confronted once again the puzzle of why it was always claimed in India that MRA was not a Christian organization. Later, I was also to discover that, by its own description in the UK, it has as its stated aim the spreading of Christianity. Why did we, as Indians, believe so naïvely, trust so blindly, and remain so childlike in our relations with this import from the West? I have heard culture defined as boundaryless and fluid compared to identity, which is inside, with connections and roots. I did not have trouble answering the question "who am I", even when in MRA. Instead, I was concerned at the inconsistencies of the worldview of human nature, the preoccupation with status that led to a lack in integrity, the conflict between values of tolerance and moderation that I had been taught in childhood, and the intolerance and excess I encountered. Above all, it seemed that, in spite of gaining independence from my immediate family, I did not have agency within my world.

Do we need a core identity? To me, it was central to my existence and my happiness. All of us have an inner world that consists of internalized objects, which are from the external world. How much choice do we exercise in this? How is this different in collective societies? And how much did my internalized colonial experience, imbibed from my parents and elders, affect my experience of MRA. In working as a psychotherapist across different cultures, I have found these same issues emerging time and again, and, in some cases, seen them resolved.

When I considered leaving MRA, it was because of the limitations of its narrow definitions of human nature, its relation with the world, and its beliefs in life and death. This inability to adjust to the available environment because of a deep, long-standing independence could also signify an unwillingness to forgo the "nourishment of latent needs deeply felt to be essential to the true development of an identity" (Erikson 1993, p. 100). This concerns a "delineation of those means of adaptation which the patient can afford to employ without losing an inner coherence". Once he knows his cure and his goal, he must become well enough to make the environment adapt to him—an intrinsic part of human adaptation, as Erikson asserts.

The greatest impact psychologically had lain in what I learnt to deny. This has been the hardest to identify. When I left, the reasons for my departure were contained in all the things MRA said it was not. The denial of our own Indian philosophical, and what counts for everyday, life made the question of identity insurmountable. Erikson describes negative identity fragments as

> self-images, even those of a highly idealistic nature, which are diametrically opposed to the dominant values of an individual's upbringing, parts of a negative identity—meaning an identity which he has been warned not to become, which he can become only with a divided heart. [1993, p. 102]

Alienation from the family was inevitable in many cases. Thankfully, in my case, I had a very instinctively supportive father and he, with reservations, made it possible for me to leave school at the age of fourteen years and work with MRA and stood by me loyally against mother, relatives, and teachers. This being India, the group of people who were concerned with my life was large and voluble. He supported and financed me.

Over the past few years, cults have acquired a malevolent reputation. People who participate are depicted as kooky, weirdoes, gullible, stupid, and deviant. Leaders of some cults have been mesmerizing, hypnotic personalities with the power to control and manipulate groups of people. We have seen the effects of propaganda that turns people into suicide bombers and killers. However, cults also exist as a default valve for what the rest of society may be lacking. They offer a community that supports the many who join them.

Modern neuropsychology provides evidence of unconscious mental processes. It can be shown that the behaviour of brain-injured patients responds to memories that are unavailable to conscious recollection. So, it is possible for brain-damaged patients to pick out people who have treated them well. We are learning that well-established distinctions between explicit and implicit memory systems remain, and non-conscious perceptual pathways have relatively direct access to the brain's emotional memory centres. We now know a good deal more about how the brain works, its processing of information, how language and memory are organized, how it solves problems and guides behaviour. But we have very little knowledge of what constitutes our sense of self. The riddle continues, and this remains the challenge to psychology. In trying to make sense of it all, I have attempted to return to the questions that sent me in the direction of this profession.

Psychotherapy offered an idea where lives could be lived to the fullest. Back in India, I had a notion of the ideas of Freud and understood that psychoanalysis offered to redeem the ill-conceived aspects of my upbringing. I grew up feeling that I was incapable of the good behaviour my sister demonstrated with such ease. Back then, it was only psychoanalysis, and I had no notion of what else existed. So, several years later, when I decided to become a therapist, I sought out a course not even knowing that there were other schools. I did a year at an established training organization in London, but felt somewhat unfulfilled when I realized that there was no awareness of differences in culture. I felt short-changed, and left to join a college closer to my home, but somewhere in my head was now lodged the idea that I would have to just follow whatever was available so as to be able to make some sort of a career. The course I embarked upon was for a diploma in counselling. At the time, the course was changing its focus from psychoanalytic to integrative, but, because none of this was evident and, to be honest, I would not have known the difference then (it is hard to imagine now how difficult these things were to ascertain at that time), I plunged headlong into it. I was engaged and stimulated. Year one was interesting and involving. By year two the course began to shift its emphasis to integrative therapy, where Petroska Clarkson's "five model" theory (Clarkson, 2002) became more firmly applied. This is based on a five-model relationship between client and therapist which brought together key aspects of different theories. Clarkson wrote, "one of the central distinguishing features of post-modernism is its distrust of the one truth or the distrust of any so called one truth" (*ibid.*, p. viii). Thus, she set about formulating a theory which encompassed aspects of different models and emphasized the "creative space between in the relationship.

Once again, I felt most drawn to the psychoanalytic component. But, more than anything, I longed for a more cultural fit. Questions arose all the time about everything. For example, early attachment patterns, so different in Indian families.

On completion of my counselling training, I was aware that something was missing. Although my training had been stimulating and absorbing, I felt that there was a void, and that my own cultural and intellectual differences had played a peripheral role in preparing me to practise in this profession. Almost always, I was the only person from another culture on these courses, and my response to the lack of any other context than Western was to constantly explain my own culture and its difference and to get exhausted in the process. Even basic concepts of congruence and the use of language needed further elaboration and were met with incomprehension and avoidance. The therapist in the first of my vignettes is myself. We were constantly urged to bring ourselves into the sessions, told that the type of relationship depended on the congruence of the therapist. But I felt very alone and compelled to present myself in language and form that made me acceptable within the Western concepts of my course. The other bits were unacceptable or incomprehensible. The fragmented bits of my personality that had first emerged in trying to be as "good" as my sister, and which later found me performing contortions to remain within a cultural context in MRA, seemed to extend to the role that my culture was playing in my profession.

When confronted with the idea of psychotherapy, Indians generally make the following points: that it is a Western construct, and therefore not relevant to Indians, or that the mix of firm religious beliefs and the extended family and supportive community provides the cushioning people need in order to resolve psychological problems, or that the Hindu concept of *moksha* (enlightenment + reincarnation) gives meaning to suffering because it leads to a higher birth in the next life, and all we can do in this life is to accept it.

Roland (1989) outlines the following overarching factors which define the Indian self:

1. The familial self.
2. The individualized self.
3. The spiritual self.
4. An expanding self.

The familial self

This is a basic inner psychological organization, predominant in India, which enables men and women to function within hierarchical relationships of the extended family, community, and other groups. These are highly personalized, extended family relationships, and are characterized by intense emotional connectedness and interdependence, with heightened asking for and giving of affection and warmth and with full expectations for reciprocity often empathetically conveyed without explicit expression. Thus, communication is always conducted on at least two levels: the nonverbal and the verbal. "Talking things over" is not the panacea in Indian relationships that it is perceived to be in the West.

In spite of being deeply enmeshed in the familial self, Indians keep a profoundly private self, where the feelings and fantasies that must be consciously contained within the etiquette of the structural relationships are kept accessible. This inner psychological space is an ego boundary. A three-dimensional model of Indians includes the ability to create an inner private space which is central to Indian individuality. When hierarchical relationships are not nurturing, this inner world may become depressed.

The Indian sense of self is less identified with work than it is with the familial self. The inner self is relational and situational.

The individualized self

Individuation takes the form of the recognition that persons have different natures. Thus, conforming to social hierarchy is balanced with expressing personal variety. Individuation also takes the form of specific occupational skills, which increasingly includes a high level of education and technological and professional skills. Where traditional skills are involved, there is closer individuation through the *jati* (kinship group), although this is changing very quickly with a burgeoning middle class and vast migration from the villages to the cities.

The spiritual self

A basic assumption in Hindu culture, the spiritual self, is deeply engraved in the preconscious of all Indians. It is present at various stages in the life cycle and is the central theme of individuation throughout life. It is the inner reality that is expressed through a complex structure of rituals and meditation and a variety of spiritual disciplines. An inner spiritual reality within everyone leads to the possibility of spiritual realization through many paths.

Many Indian men and women maintain a constant surveillance for the clairvoyant, telepathic, or the prophetic as part of a profound concern with destiny. In the Hindu view of things, attachments from past lives, cosmic influences, and unconscious motivations and fantasies are all related with present-day relationships. Hindu psychology links unconscious fantasies from childhood and present-day relationships with cosmic influences and attachments from past lives.

The expanded self

Indians are exposed to conflicting value systems and world-views, to significantly different ways of social relatedness and life styles, and to different modes of psychological functioning. Further complicating the identity integrations was the incorporation of the

> constant British deprecation of everything Indian. Thus the need for an identity synthesis is not within the core self, as it is for Westerners, but rather between the core self and various aspects of acculturation to Western culture, tremendously conflicted by British devaluation of the indigenous self. [Kakar, 1978, p. 67]

Kakar (1978) argues that, deep down, Western-educated Indian men and women must to this day make a decisive choice between being Indian in identity or Western. Whenever the identity investment is more Western, there is inevitably a subtle or open denigration of many things Indian. The layering nature of culture and religion frequently show up in the Indian self, where indigenous culture is assumed as integrated at an earlier, emotional level and Western culture on a later, cognitive level. The integrations of new cultural ideals such as competitive achievement with the old ones of maintaining *jati* integrity have fostered an expanding self that is adrift.

I finally found my professional home after many years of training when I undertook the MSc in Psychoanalytic Psychotherapy in intercultural therapy at Nafsiyat/University College London. With its feet firmly in contemporary anthropology, the study of psychoanalysis provided the broadest base from which to provide therapy across cultures. Intercultural therapy addresses all issues of difference. Nafsiyat Intercultural Therapy Centre was founded to provide the best therapy to those in society who could least afford it.

Your reflection

- Consider a moment in your therapy training when you felt "different" to others. Try to capture a situation and a feeling and write the experience of "clashing" cultures.

CHAPTER EIGHT

Susan's story: working with the beyond

Introduction to transpersonal psychology

Transpersonal psychology has been around since the mid 1960s. It is informed by psychoanalytical, psychodynamic, gestalt, and person-centred thinking, but includes a spiritual dimension to growth. This means that higher energies such as intuition, inspiration, altruism, artistic inclination, and a connection to something beyond the personal self are actively included. Spirituality was traditionally regarded by Freud as regressive, but developed by Jung as an innate and vital force pulling us towards growth, meaning, and humility. It allows us to move beyond our own self-absorption and find our appropriate place in the scheme of all that is. It seems particularly relevant in the twenty-first century, where a lot of the trappings of the cult of the personality are failing, such as rampant capitalism, squandering of the environment, self-interest, and instant gratification.

Maslow put self-actualization at the top of his hierarchy of needs, and the traits of a person who had reached this pinnacle of development was a sense of personal richness with a good enough relationship with self and others, but, in addition, a connection with a power beyond themselves which is an integral part of transpersonal psychology.

Psychosynthesis is a specific model within the transpersonal umbrella, and the main thrust is synthesizing or harmonizing all of the component parts of the person, both egoic and spiritual, around the core essence. Resolving and integrating childhood wounding takes equal standing to integrating peak experiences that go beyond the personal realm and give a taste of the transpersonal world. Many clients who are attracted to psychosynthesis may have had transpersonal experiences that they need to explore and find meaning from. Psychosynthesis endeavours to include the wisdom and experiences of sages and mystics from down the ages, but combines this with rigorous psychological enquiry. It is about both the traditionally psychological and innately spiritual.

There had been a series of significant events that had led me to study psychosynthesis. On a counselling skills course, I was intrigued by the work of Jung. Although I had abandoned my Catholic faith long ago, I found myself drawn to the ideas of a spiritual nature that Jung seemed to hint at. At the same time, I was recommended two books that helped me understand: one was *Further Along the Road Less Travelled*, by Scott Peck, and the other was *Conversations with God*, by Neale Donald Walsh. I was encouraged by Scott Peck's idea about a combined spiritual and psychological development. His hypothesis that there is a step after abandonment of organized religion that includes a personal relationship with the divine really resonated with me. I had always assumed that if you did not accept religion there was nowhere else to go. So I was intrigued and excited. *Conversations with God* helped me re-establish the personal connection with the divine and my own spiritual nature. Therefore, the process of studying psychosynthesis, which I was introduced to around this transformational time, ran in parallel with my spiritual re-awakening, and one facilitated the other.

Beyond the personal

The main thrust of transpersonal therapy is that it goes beyond the personal. It includes exploration of our divine nature as well as the personality, and contends that the two are inextricably linked. It assumes that we have an innate drive for growth and evolution. It views life challenges as fuel for transformation. Higher aspects, such as love, joy, beauty, and peace, as well as aspects of our shadowy side, such as anger, jealousy, and vengeance, are all grist for the mill of personal development. Transpersonal therapy is guided by the inspiring progressive view that we are more than our pathology and that we are always in the process of growth and fulfilling our potential.

Seeking therapy

As part of the requirement of my course I needed to be in therapy with a psychosynthesis therapist, and I was able to find someone locally. I started eagerly wanting to find myself, although deep down inside I was sure there was really nothing very much to learn and that I had a strong sense of self and a firm grasp on reality. I was only going into therapy because it was a requirement of my course. It took me several years to really peel away the layers and to find my insecurities, my shadow, my longings and desires, my depression, and my madness. However, I did find all these things and more, and was shocked and surprised in equal measure. How can all of that be contained in one human? I was humbled by the process and feel grateful that I have had the resources to pursue my self-development. I am proud that I was able to get past my defences and really engage with the process and, although I did not always like what I discovered, I do own it as part of me. I also see it as a work in progress and a lifetime's journey.

Training to work as a therapist

Training to be a psychosynthesis therapist was very rewarding. It is predominantly an experiential course. There was a thematic weekend every month on skills, the body, sexuality, pathology, creative visualization, childhood, creative use of pain, crisis, and failure. It was about using your self as a laboratory for growth and development, leading to a deep understanding of what is required for self development and healing. Although a high academic standard was required, for me it was the personal commitment and involvement that seemed critical. We could not expect our clients to go within to any place we had not been ourselves, which seems a sound philosophy to me, but I am also aware that it is less of a requirement in many training organizations today.

As with any good training, the motives for becoming a therapist are also important to meditate on. What is it that motivates individuals to train and become therapists? As with many things in life, it is usually a mix of conscious and unconscious forces. We may know consciously that we want to make a difference, help people who are suffering, give something back, but are we aware that alongside this can be unconscious needs to feel more powerful, rescue others so we can feel better about ourselves, give what we really need ourselves to others in the hope that somehow it will come back, repeat a childhood pattern of being the carer, because that was the role assigned to us in the family? If these dynamics have not been healed, then repetitive compulsion will require that we repeat them until some resolution is achieved. There is a danger that they are repeated between the therapist and a client, and that a collusion is set up which is an impediment to growth and progress.

If this grandiosity is not brought into awareness and worked through, it is possible that the therapist can be a danger to themselves and others. To highlight this, I would like to bring in an experience that shocked me into consciousness about this process. I did a placement in an agency that rented rooms in a church hall. I would be referred clients and see them on my own in the church hall with no one backing me up. It had never occurred to me to question the safety of this set up. I was in denial that in helping someone I could be putting myself in danger. I was a therapist and in charge and in control. My work was above the petty considerations of safety. It was higher work! My first client was a very distressed middle-aged man, and several weeks into our work he confided that he had been in prison for grievous bodily harm. He had not mentioned this in the assessment with my colleague and I suddenly felt very afraid, alone, and vulnerable. Where had been my concerns for myself; what did this tell me about my need to deny any of my own requirements and see only the client as in need of help and understanding? Soon after this, another incident shocked me even more. I approached the same venue with the key to unlock the door and saw a shadowy figure moving inside the building. I was about to walk in on a robbery. Luckily, I moved away and phoned the police. I learnt my lesson very well, and luckily with no personal consequences, but I never will put myself in that dangerous position again and I know that not everyone can be helped and that my needs and safety are also paramount.

I think it is usual that after the initial euphoria of finding therapy and training and doing the work, apathy can set in. Why am I doing this work is a common question, and I have certainly asked it many times over the years. If I am just repeating childhood patterns, then what is the point? I feel that a period of doubt and reflection periodically is an important part of the recommitment process, or may result in the work as a therapist ending and another chapter beginning. For me, I have been in that place several times now over the years, and I have always decided to continue so far. Each cycle has led to a deeper understanding of what the work is and what is required, and it has resulted in a deepening of my work with others. I also know that one day it may mean I stop practising, and so be it. You have to be able to say no to this work before you can fully say yes. It also seems to me to be like a relationship; you get into it without full awareness of everything that motivates you, but it is an opportunity and a catalyst for those dynamics to surface and heal and for a purer engagement with the work to emerge as a result. The unconscious dynamics that steer us to this work are not the full story; they are the preamble, and beneath this is a motivation of pure intent that is always in the process of being uncovered. It feels like a trap to me to stop once the apathetic phase has been reached, in the same way that relationships do not have to end when the honeymoon period is over. It is an opportunity for a recommitment from a different place, and that opens up unimagined vistas. If this is your destiny, then you have to stick at it no matter what and, at the same time, not get attached to doing it at all. Good luck.

Working as a therapist

My area of interest is higher education. I work in a university setting with students and staff. The staff work is predominantly adult, one-to-one work, although I also do some couples work. The student work also involves awareness of the particular aspect of late adolescence. For many students, it is the first time they have lived away from home, and so separation anxiety can be an overwhelming dynamic, even though the young people are choosing to do it and happy about leaving home. They are called upon to make sense of their unique family of origin experiences and dynamics to find a sense of themselves separate from their families and to go out into the world. For most, this process goes smoothly, but some experience problems such as depression, loneliness, and homesickness. Similarly, if they have a mental health issue, such as Asberger's, autism, or an eating disorder, it can become exacerbated because of the strain on their already barely adequate defences. If there are problems at home, the student can be unavailable to their academic and social life at university, because emotionally they are still at home in the family system and this usually leads to a sense of not being able to settle or engage with university life. However, it is rewarding and stimulating work, which is never dull. It is about working with what comes up in the session, although there is a lot of backup available from tutors, doctors, and care services, so it rarely feels as if I am alone with the client and the issues. It is general practice, and it suits me well.

Case study

I would like to present a case study from one of my university clients.

Endurance: getting the clients you need

Amy is a Korean student and had already been attending the centre for some time, and was now using it as a drop-in centre when she needed a space to talk. I found myself sitting in front of her and feeling an intense irritation, but also a heart-sinking feeling that nothing could be done.

I should also mention that I felt uneasy about working with Amy. The truth was that I had spent five years of my life living in Korea, returning to the UK ten years previously. It is a time that I describe as "wilderness years", because of the unhappiness and, at times, desolation that I felt during that period. From the distance of time, and having afterwards trained as a therapist, with all the reflection and awareness that brings, I knew the experience had been the making of me. I was thrown back on myself because of the isolation of my circumstances and the language barrier to such an extent that I had no choice but to dig deep and find a sense of myself within. However, this process was far from easy, and left me with a bittersweet and rather suspicious sense of Korean culture and people. Could I overcome this and work with Amy?

She talked about her life and how it had been blighted by a deep depression that she could not remember being free of. At adolescence, she tried to kill herself several times before being referred to a psychiatrist who was a colleague of her father. Her father was a revered and successful surgeon in Korea. I could only imagine the sense of shame she must have internalized because of her letting the family down.

Our initial sessions were stilted and awkward because of her limited English and my Scottish accent, which led to a lot of confusion and misunderstanding. She evoked many things in me, including rage, particularly at her passiveness. I wanted shot of her as quickly as possible. There was also, at times, the most disabling fog in my brain that made it impossible to think and that made me want to sleep the sleep of the dead. It was a paralysing, trance-inducing state that was neither alive nor dead, but suspended somewhere in between. I felt her communicate through this fog her inner world, and I sensed how difficult it must be to operate with this hanging over her. It was little surprise to me that she talked about a troubled childhood, had few friends, and rarely went out, but had a history of being bullied that made her withdraw even more, which compounded her sense of being an outcast. She regularly talked about life being joyless, and that she had no hope that it could be otherwise.

It would have been so easy for me to find an excuse to stop working with Amy. Our mode, at the university, is shorter term, solution focused for the most part, with a small proportion of clients being offered longer-term work. I was not convinced that Amy could use what I had to offer, and resources were tight. However, something nagged at the back of my mind and I was suspicious of my lack of concern for this young woman who was enduring life until she could die. Why did I not feel more compassion?

I resolved to present her at our clinical meeting, with the hope that my colleagues would back me up and that I could stop working with her. They saw through my lame excuses and there was a turning point when one of my colleagues said that she had worked with a Korean student and it was more about befriending rather than thinking therapeutically and that my expectations of her may be too high. This had been how her parents had treated her, and I realized how much I was playing out her life pattern. I committed to our work together and we started seeing each other weekly with a view to medium-term work.

It was slow, tedious work, and we spent many sessions just chatting and passing time. In the spirit of befriending, which I had decided was the best course, I shared that I had lived in Korea. Self-disclosure is not something I necessarily do, but with Amy it felt right and gave me a sense of freedom in my work that I did not usually have. Our sessions, at times, had a cultural exchange quality, which was not therapy in the traditional sense, but, in hindsight, helped to build our relationship. At times, I was aware of what a unique match we were, since I had an insight into her culture that was unusual for a Westerner (if, at times, critical) and at many points there was an understanding that someone who had not lived in Korea would not have had, but, equally, I was not Korean, so I was not making assumptions that perhaps someone with the same upbringing may have done. At times in my therapy career, I have been aware of the perfect synchronicity of the clients that have found their way to me and have heard this shared by colleagues too. Amy was one of those clients. We were made for each other.

There were times when I dreaded her coming because of the mind fog that we both viewed each other through. When she talked about not being able to focus on work or retain information or think straight, I knew exactly what she was talking about because that is how I felt when I was in the room with her. This projective identification was very debilitating and I could do nothing but hang on. I endeavoured to feed back to her how I experienced her and the impact her state of mind would have on her studies. I encouraged her to be compassionate with herself, but she was much happier retaining her view that she was not good enough or hard-working enough, and that she must redouble her efforts. In time, I did not dread her coming and actually felt free in our sessions, because I had no attachment to what might happen. I started to feel affectionate towards her but still, if I am honest, not much of a sense of compassion for her suffering. I wondered if she had any compassion for herself?

In parallel with her journey I was taking a journey of my own back to Korea and to some of the difficult times I had experienced there. I had arrived in Korea in April 1993, eight months married and five months pregnant. I was twenty-nine, and felt I had the world at my feet. I was in for a rude awakening, and, looking back, I think I was naïve in thinking that I could cope with every change possible being thrown at me at once. Needless to say, I did not cope. Everything came to a head with the birth of my first son, which is a challenge at the best of times, but in a different culture, no language skills, new house, new job, with a husband preoccupied with his job and learning Korean in an intense immersion course, and everything alien, I quickly sank into a depression of my own that I did not have the life experience or internal resources to fathom or the wherewithal to seek help.

This anger at being marooned in a country that I did not understand at a vulnerable time of my life was reawakened in my work with Amy. I felt I was quick to judge her and her culture, which I did not voice directly, but perhaps in subtle ways I encouraged her to explore the impact her culture limitations had on her mental health. I could tell by her responses when I was coming from my need to feel superior and for revenge, as she would withdraw and become passive and I would get infuriated. However, in time, this fell away, and we very slowly and subtly started relating on a human-to-human level. She revealed more of herself, and talk about her struggles and my dread of our sessions became less. The reparative process was operating almost imperceptibly and almost despite us.

Important core aspects of the psychosynthesis model were key in my work with Amy. Non-attachment to outcome was particularly important. I was forced to confront and put aside my need for Amy to make progress and allow her to develop at her pace and in her own way. This did not mean that I did not care for her or her life challenges, but that I needed to get myself out of the way so that she could find what was important for her.

The experiences that united us, rather than divided us, became more obvious to me. We both had an experience of a deep sense of isolation, failure, and doom, which disabled our thinking capacity. We both knew what it was like to find ourselves in a world of which we could no longer make sense. Looking back, I could find no words to explain or find meaning in my experiences. A sense of desolation, wretchedness, hopelessness, and no way out descended on me at a time I was told was the best of my life. Amy was a young, attractive, bright woman with everything to live for, and yet life was wretched, a constant struggle.

However, working with Amy really made me assess my experience in Korea in a different light. My initial memories were negative, but the more I reflected on them, and with a decade of distance between myself and the unhappy time, I began to see the gift. It was almost as if I had gone on an extended retreat and emerged much stronger, more aware of myself and others. It was also in Korea that I was introduced to counselling through a Samaritans-like helpline for foreigners. I trained to become a telephone counsellor, and found the focus on emotional understanding and awareness so refreshing and such an antidote to my scientific training that I had had as an undergraduate. I felt I had entered a whole new world and it inspired me. I resolved to train as a therapist when I returned to the UK. I feel strongly that my experiences in Korea were exactly what I needed to grow and find a more meaningful purpose in my life, and that there was an intelligence to it even if at times I was not aware of it. In fact, I felt abandoned rather than supported, but, looking back, the transpersonal was working through me to draw out the exact experiences I needed to grow. My work with Amy really helped me know this.

In one pivotal session with Amy, we were talking of her adolescence and her suicide attempts. I cannot actually remember what I had asked her, but I was aware of feeling an availability and receptivity to her that embodied the elusive qualities of "presence", which I will expand on later. Her response shocked and surprised me.

She said, "My life ended then", and with the word "then" she emphatically brought her left hand firmly down on to the palm of her right hand in a chopping movement.

I was taken aback by the harsh, defiant tone of her voice. The anger it portrayed was something I had felt very strongly in our sessions but had never seen her express. Her lips were curled into a twisted knot through which she spat these words out. It was a part of her that I had never seen.

We both sat in stunned silence.

Very quickly, I felt flooded with grief. Tears welled up in my eyes and I struggled to contain inside myself what felt uncontainable. A voice inside my head said, "Let her see your tears". I finally had a deep sense of compassion for Amy that had been conspicuous by its absence in our work together but which now flooded in. I was very touched, which seemed like a breakthrough even at the time. Being tearful in front of clients, along with self-disclosure and touching, are aspects of therapy that are endlessly debated and the impact on clients endlessly discussed, but, as with other aspects of my work with Amy, I was challenged to take a path that I would not normally take and I let her see my tears. My instincts seemed to tell me this was what was right, and I trusted that. At times in therapy, we have to make instantaneous decisions about how we are with a client, and although it is important to keep the internal supervisor actively involved and weighing up what is best for the client, at other times the process guides you rather than the other way around.

Psychosynthesis hypothesizes that we have an "I", which is our divine essence beyond but also including our conditioning and wounding. It is our true self (as opposed to the false self) which we are always in the process of becoming and which Maslow was hinting at in the term "self-actualizing" in his hierarchy of needs. I am struck with the idea that therapy is not just about reducing anxiety or psychological symptoms, but about fulfilling potential and helping us to engage fully with all life has to offer from an authentic place. I endeavour, in my work with clients, to see past the story they bring and that, at times, they completely identify with. It is not about disregarding their story, but about including that they are more than their history and how they present. Each is a unique being with the potential for growth and fulfilment. This is termed bifocal vision, and describes well the stance that the therapist could take in being with a client.

During this encounter with Amy, there was a sacred moment when she showed me how it really was for her on the inside and I was also holding her ability to heal and to integrate her earlier traumatic experiences. It was not consciously willed on her part, and, equally, there was a receptive part in me that was a witness to her story but could also sense the deeper essence underneath. The process seemed to be bigger than us, and we both felt the significance of it. A force working through us both that cannot be faked or pushed, but, when it occurs, it is profoundly significant. In truth, it was very uncomfortable for me, and she was also visibly uncomfortable.

I would love to say that from this moment Amy was changed for ever, and went on to a fulfilled and happy life, but the truth is she did not, and she still struggles daily with a chronic depression and she is still ambivalent about being alive, and so our work continues. However, she is at times more engaged and is aware of her ambivalence, and with these slow baby steps she is getting to know herself and her challenges better.

Therapists' use of self in transpersonal therapy

Within this section I would like to outline my thoughts about the therapists' use of self within the context of transpersonal therapy. The transpersonal school evolved to include the spiritual dimensions of the human condition, that is, that which goes beyond the personal or personality. It hypothesizes that there is an organizing principle which guides our growth on a personal level, helping us to evolve to higher levels of consciousness. Growth does not stop with the disappearance of symptoms, but is a lifetime's journey going deeper and higher into our true essence.

All mystical traditions include the hypotheses of an ultimate reality that interconnects us; a divinity with a scope that is unfathomable to the logical rational mind, but which has more to do with a subtle realm that we all sense and know in our deeper essence. The egoic rational, particularly Western, mind would persuade us out of this truth, but, as mentioned in Rowan and Jacobs' book *The Therapist's Use of Self* (2002), "You cannot know ultimate reality, you have to become it".

What is the relevance of ultimate reality to the therapeutic process? It seems to me that therapy takes place on many levels simultaneously. All therapists would surely agree that attention to appropriate boundaries and knowing clearly where one person stops and the therapist begins is one of the foundations of safe, ethical, contained work. However, therapy is also about tolerating paradox and authentic open relating, bringing all of the aspects of the human condition to the service of the soul. At the same time as the therapist is attending to the client on a personality or ordinary consciousness level, there is also always the opportunity for boundaries to dissolve and for two souls to meet and to draw on something beyond and bigger than them both, thus entering the realm of expanded or altered states of consciousness.

As far-fetched and challenging as this may sound, it does not take too much searching of the therapy literature to find quotes from all schools of therapy that allude to this remarkable meeting and the positive impact on both client and therapist. This is not a phenomenon reserved solely for the transpersonal practitioner, although the transpersonal school may have tried to incorporate it actively within its model. Is this perhaps the I–Thou relating that Buber (1946) alludes to? Rowan and Jacobs (2002) outline this phenomenon from many schools of therapy, with phrases like "relational depth", "in-between state", "conjunctio", "absolute self-forgetfulness". As I hope is clear, this is not an unheard of phenomenon, and not strictly reserved to the transpersonal school, but is available to individuals who are curious, courageous, and committed to expanding the frontiers of therapy beyond the egoic separateness that we have come to know as self.

"Presence" is a common factor in all of the descriptions of expanded consciousness. Being truly present seems to be a catalyst for the opening up of these subtle realms. What is "presence"? Again, all mystical traditions talk of and teach the theory of presence as a prerequisite, although not a guarantee, of expanded consciousness. To be fully present to the self is to be in the moment, aware, connected, alert, centred, and open to the subtle realms. There is an attitude of inner surrender, but also of alert aliveness that, once experienced, is never forgotten. It is, perhaps, not possible to live in this place, but in order for the boundaries to fall between the therapist and client, the more present the therapist can be the better. This is not a technique that can be learnt or forced, but, rather, allowed. It is more a letting go and surrender than an active doing of anything. The more work the therapist has done on his or her issues, the more the blocks to safe dissolution of boundaries are mediated. It is the firming of ego boundaries through self-knowledge and awareness, paradoxically, that allow them to fall away and re-establish without problems. The phrase "you have to become somebody before you can become nobody" sums this up perfectly, or, put another way, "the path to sainthood has to pass through adulthood".

These altered states do not come without a word of warning. The ecstatic nature of them makes them very attractive, and the human condition is such that we want the good stuff with, perhaps, the least amount of effort or pain. If the ego strength through which the states are accessed is not strong enough, then the danger is that instead of progressing to higher states of consciousness, there is a regression to pre-egoic states that can lead to psychotic breakdown, with all that that entails. John Nelson, in his book *Healing the Split* (1991), goes into great detail on the difference. One is expanded and feels manageable, the other is paranoid and unmanageable. Within the client–therapist relationship, however, this can be avoided through long-term therapy and regular supervision and continuous professional development. It is my belief and experience that there is a self-regulating aspect to these states, and that the depth achieved is that which is manageable by the parties involved.

I have briefly outlined my views on the therapist's use of self, using a transpersonal lens. I have mentioned the subtle realm, or ultimate reality, that can be evoked in the room between a client and a therapist: a sacred space with which deeper, more meaningful connection and authentic relating can take place. I like to think that, in our true essence, we all yearn for a more authentic connection with our fellow travellers, and that therapy may be one of the last places left to us in Western culture where we can do this. The healing potential of such an experience should not be under-estimated, and can sustain us long after the experience has passed. It nourishes both the client and the therapist, and supports not only authentic relating between them, but also with the self.

Your reflection

- Can you think of challenging experiences in your own life that, in time, have given way to insight about yourself, life situation, or work?

CHAPTER NINE

Pam's story. Design or destiny:
what brings us to therapy and
the place of the self and possible
self-disclosure in the therapeutic
alliance

From the seeds of our small writing group emerged the idea of exploring how it was we came to be therapists.

So, one quiet morning, I sat and wrote. Aside from writing for my past academic studies, I am not a "writer" and had little self-belief in my ability to do so. Images of returned essays with red pen comments and disappointing marks were not far away as I began . . .

It was a cathartic experience, both moving and revealing, and some of it I shared with the group. Then came the realization that our writing could be published and a part of me would be laid bare to a very public audience, including my clients, and how this would or could potentially affect existing relationships, both personal and professional.

My past is not dramatic; it is not tantalizingly interesting, as this might make it sound. It is a past mottled with experiences, many good ones, and some extremely difficult and painful.

This is where it becomes hard. Painful and difficult experiences are rarely experienced in isolation away from others. In fact, it is very often the relational dynamics, both of the past and the present, that can orchestrate a rupture, a trauma, so any self-revelation usually involves other people who may well not wish to be part of any confessional testimony.

I guess if I could use one word to describe what brought me to be a therapist it would be *loss* in its many guises, but this is where, for me, any further detail of sharing my personal story with a wider audience has to end. However, what is indicative from this is my inherent interest in self-disclosure, which has been there from the start of my career as a trainee therapist right through to the present. It is the subject I chose to research for my Masters dissertation.

Much of my story I have shared with some good friends and my family. I have also taken a lot of my story, and "myself" to personal therapy. The latter, of course, has been a place shielded by confidentiality, congruence, and a non-judgemental arena. Humanistically, I had a companion who formed a therapeutic relationship built on Rogerian core conditions. Existentially, I have had a companion who was able to sit with me and share my silence: my "dread" that at times I had no voice or words to express or even know what my dread was. Psychoanalytically, I had a companion who could analyse and interpret. It was a space that was mine, where I did not have to worry about the other or what affect my words, or silence, might have on the other, or, indeed, what the other had experienced. As a client in therapy, it is a unique and very special place to be.

Such a space is so special and so unique and really, until experienced, is hard to explain. For me, that place was, and remains, a very challenging, yet very safe place.

All of us know how difficult it can be to share our inner concerns at times with close members of our family, because they are often involved, or certainly have a subjective view on the matter, and the same applies to our friends. Equally, we often know parts of "their" stories that, without doubt, affect the way we tell our own narrative or the freedom we can allow ourselves do so.

I have often reflected, like many, as to what brought me to be a therapist. Has it been by design, or was it my destiny, or are the two irrevocably linked? I also wonder what brings one person to one therapist, given the amount of therapists practising in a given area, and what role serendipity plays.

I am an *integrative therapist*. This choice was not made initially with any researched knowledge base. I went to a six-week introductory course in counselling, run by the local university, and this fed into the Masters course, which I subsequently attended. The training focused on the experiential and phenomenological, and taught me the "basics" of some of the major influences that form the backbone to different therapeutic practices.

We looked at Rogers and the person-centred approach, psycho-analysis, existentialism, and postmodernism. Our own personal therapy and supervision *had* to be with psychoanalytic practition-ers, and the academic staff, on the whole, was from this school of thought and training. Interestingly, however, those who completed this course cannot be classified as "psychoanalytic practitioners" themselves.

On the completion of my course, I suppose I felt confused: a "jack of many trades but master of none". Initially, I felt envious of those soaked in the confidence of a "particular" modality, those who solely practised from a psychodynamic, or psychoanalytic, or systemic, or humanistic school of thought.

However, over the years, and with many hours of practice under my belt, I have come as a practitioner to feel, in Dido's words, "safe in my own skin". It is as though the integrative approach of a diverse backbone of different schools of thought has been like some topical balm that has slowly penetrated from the skin surface to the blood, and I am now able to feel the strength of this as I work with my clients. I feel able to draw deeply on the roots of this integrative-based training and find different sources and ways to feed and sustain the very diverse, troubled, needy, and "hungry" clients who come to see me.

A client I have worked with for a long time holds a very special place in my own road to self-awareness; a road that I constantly tread and, unlike a view held by some, has no ending. This client is from the Hindu faith and has allowed me the rare and enormous privilege of her insight into her religion and her culture, to be a part of her journey.

As I have understood her faith through her eyes, it seems that, for her, we are here on this earth having already journeyed here before, having already met in a former life many of the people we meet in this one, and for every new person we meet there is a reason.

My own understanding of this "meeting" has come to represent for me the "union" with an "*other*". This could be as simple as something felt and/or shared in a sigh, in a tear, in a smile, in a sorrow, in a glance, in a moment, but somehow in the meeting of two people.

The therapeutic alliance emerges from the strength and depth of a personal interaction built between two people. From a humanistic, Rogerian modality, this is built on trust, empathy, unconditional positive regard, and congruence.

Existentially, Heidegger's notion was that *Dasein*'s "Being is Being with", implying, as I comprehend it, that our existence in the world involves our relationships and experiences of being with others, "our relatedness".

Medard Boss, in Friedman (1999, p. 427), wrote, "The world of man's being in the world is ever primordially one which I share with others. The world of Dasein is essentially Mitwelt".

So, what is this unique relationship of therapist and client where one party "shares" and another seemingly will not, should not, or . . . perhaps does?

Do we as therapists "share " (self-disclose) with our clients? What, if anything, would we share, and what, fundamentally, is sharing in the context of the therapist to the client, since sharing implies a two-way relationship? After all, the client seems to share very much with us.

Depending on one's therapeutic model, stance, and training, the idea of "self-disclosure" in the therapeutic alliance remains firmly in the arena of debate and, to some extent, the jury remains out. Some therapists would confirm that they do "share", or, put another way, "self-disclose"; some say they never do.

Certainly, in the historical framework of psychotherapy, self-disclosure is still very much in its infancy, especially with the predominance up to the 1970s of psychoanalytical and behavioural schools of therapy. Probably up to this point, any disclosure by the therapist of personal information about himself or herself was considered inappropriate (Auvil & Silver, 1984; Jacobs, 1999).

With the Rogerian and humanistic movement (Rogers, 1951, 1961), and the later feminist movement (Brown & Walker, 1990), differing views began to emerge. Self-disclosure gradually came to be seen as part of the therapeutic relationship, considered in terms of congruence, transparency, and authenticity. Simi and Mahalik (1997) argued that, for the feminists, it was considered as a route to an egalitarian therapeutic relationship. Without doubt, if it is viewed as a technique, as Hanson (2003) emphasizes, "it can be used skillfully or unskillfully, appropriately or inappropriately", and there are risks.

In order to perhaps understand this, an explanation of what could be meant by self-disclosure is pertinent.

From my study of this subject (Critchley, 2006) I came to understand the concept in a way expressed by Knox, Hess, Peterson, and (1997, p. 274), where self-disclosing and self-involving: the *inter*personal and *intra*personal, are considered as ". . . An interaction in which the therapist reveals personal information about him/herself, and or reveals reactions and responses to the client as they arise in the session".

"*Inter*personal" here refers to the therapist revealing feelings evoked by the client, in contrast to *intra*personal, where the therapist discloses information about his or her present and past that is outside the therapy room. This is highlighted in the writing of Nilsson, Strassberg, and Bannon (1979).

It is the difference Watchel (1993) described from "session reactions" to "disclosure of personal reactions", but, at times, seemingly intertwined, as the vignettes later in this chapter suggest.

It seems that the therapist can self-disclose in different ways and on different levels. I am aware, from my own private practice, of very subtle disclosures of my lifestyle that are first experienced by potential clients when they make the first contact. My voice on the phone has been commented on by a number of clients.

My office phone is a fixed phone, and sits alongside my home phone. I remember speaking with a nervous young man enquiring about therapy when the house phone started to ring. He nervously asked, "Should you get that?'; "No," I replied, "don't worry, it will stop." It did stop, only to be immediately replaced by my mobile going off (the ring tone, incidentally, set by my children to a very loud setting as a result of their frustration with my not hearing it!). At this point in the conversation I started to laugh, apologizing to the enquiring client for the background interruptions. He subsequently came for therapy and stayed with me for a number of years, and he commented quite early on about what a relief it had been that day to hear me laugh and realize that I was human. Another example was a lady also enquiring about coming to see me and being most relieved when I could not find my glasses to enable me to look at dates in my diary: "Thank goodness it isn't only me," she said. She, too, came, and stayed in long-term therapy.

When clients arrive for therapy, which is at my home, I have also often wondered what clients make of the array of cars that at times sit on our drive . . . one male client was certainly interested in a new car (my husband's) that arrived and was amused at my total lack of knowledge about it, but found this a useful way to start our therapy sessions, relaxing him initially. Now, after numerous sessions, he no longer needs "the prop".

I have a piano in my consulting room and this, too, is an interesting focus. Questions do arise as to whether I play, and I am very conscious of putting away any music, as this could indeed self-disclose an awful lot about me and or my mood!

So, knowingly or unknowingly, we disclose from the onset of the first contact, in the following ways.

- Our website style or voice as we answer the phone.
- Our geographical location.
- Those in private practice who work from home disclose their house, indications of wealth/status . . . cars in the drive.
- Choices of furnishings, decorations, etc. maybe the tell-tale signs of other occupants in the house, or pets.
- Our dress, our style, our manner, all disclose something to the "other".
- Wedding rings, photographs.
- Our professional qualifications and training.

In my study (Critchley, 2006, p. 25), citing Weiner (1983),

> self disclosure is described as the therapist giving more than just professional expertise or when the therapist is more open and genuine with the client. Such (self-disclosing) openness includes the therapist revealing feelings, attitudes, opinions, associations, experiences or history.

Certainly, some of the literature (Knox, Hess, Peterson, & Hill, 1997) on self-disclosure places a distinction between the therapist *revealing personal information* to a client and the therapist *revealing personal experience* to the client in the therapeutic setting. Hill and

Knox (2001) later expand on this with their reference defining self-disclosure as "non-immediate revelations about personal information, in contrast to immediate revelations of feelings within the therapeutic alliance" (Critchley, 2006, p. 26).

Wells (1994) had earlier made the same distinction, outlining the four definitions of self-disclosure as:

(i)   Professional qualifications, training and experience;
(ii) Any *personal information*, both circumstances and experiences disclosed to the client;
(iii) Disclosure of *personal feelings* aroused by the client in the therapeutic alliance, both positive and negative;
(iv) *Admission*, discussion, possible apology to client for *mistakes* made by the therapist in the therapeutic session (Critchley, 2006, p. 26; see also, Casement, 2002, p. 32).

Experience has shown me, though, that at times the edges between (ii) and (iii) from the above can become confused and blurred. Very recently, a new client came and began to explain about the effects of a chronic medical condition she has. Unknown to her, I, too, suffer with this condition. It was, for me, an extraordinary session. I gained so much from it to hear first-hand how it was for another, how reassuring and comforting, and also educating. To date, I have told her nothing of my shared condition. I believe my empathy was massively in the room, but at the moment I do not feel it would be helpful for her to (i) *know*, or for her to know (ii) the *feelings* I experienced in the session, although, interestingly, I have wondered, having read Francesca's case study (pp. 88–92), whether it would be helpful for her to know, and if, indeed, she finds out at some later stage whether she might feel angry, hurt, or confused about the fact that I did not self-disclose.

My reasons for not either disclosing the fact that I have this condition, or my experience in the session, are that she is currently overwhelmed by her symptoms and she needs an exclusive place for these to be voiced and her pain contained and held, and not shared, or any sense of having to worry about me. My supervisor agrees.

So, what of the boundaries and the ethical implications of disclosure and possible benefits and or risks?

In my study (Critchely, 2006, p. 28), I note:

The benefits discussed in the literature for self-disclosure are many and varied (Ackerman & Hisenroth, 2001; Auvil & Silver, 1984; Bridges, 2001; Jacobs, 1999; Knox, Hess, Peterson, & Hill, 1997; Simon, 1988). Hanson (2003), citing many of the above references, suggests that the following could be seen as some of the benefits of self-disclosure:

- Promotes a more egalitarian relationship;
- Advances client autonomy;
- Normalises the therapist;
- Helps in modelling or skill training, demonstrating problem solving and coping skills, provides examples of handling and surviving difficulties;
- Promotes self-awareness, self-acceptance and assertiveness;
- Facilitates client self disclosure, insight and learning;
- Helps validate and normalise client's experiences;
- Acts as a catharsis, helping client connect, discover and share emotions that have previously been withheld;
- Supports reinforcement and validation for the client;
- Enables client to make informed decision as:

"Some authors believe that clients, as consumers, have a right to know therapist's values, positions, views or experience" (Hanson, 2003).

In respect of risk, Peterson (2002) argues the importance of non-maleficence and beneficience, meaning that, as a therapist, there is the need to avoid doing any harm to clients and that the therapist's aim is to help others, so, if self-disclosing, then the therapist's action must in no way violate these.

Peterson (2002) and Goldstein (1994) recognize that some clients would be affected detrimentally by the therapist's use of self-disclosure, and that this might indeed violate the principle of non-maleficence.

Such clients included those with poor boundaries, poor reality testing, those who focus on others' needs rather than their own, those who fear closeness, those who are very self absorbed, and those who are trying to avoid strong emotions. Further caution is expressed for those working with children, when *avoidance* of disclosure might be harmful. Papouchis (1990, cited in Peterson, 2002), argues that avoidance of children's questions could interfere with the child mastering reality. At the other end of the age spectrum, Greenberg (1990, cited in Peterson, 2002), cautions against disclosure with the elderly, fearing that the often social isolation of the elderly could replace the role of therapist with one of intimate friend (p. 33).

Bridges (2001, p. 2) suggests that self disclosure is important in that it

> . . . facilitates exploration, introduces new perspectives on the self in a relationship, and conveys to the patient the possibility of creating a new healing object relationship. Therapist self disclosure may be a helpful vehicle to make conscious unconscious affect or relational dynamics that influence the treatment and benefit to the patient's development. [Critchley, 2006, p. 27]

So, what of our unconscious in this interaction? What Freud called countertransference.

Freud, as early as 1910, commented on the presence of countertransference and initially was clear that any such feelings evoked should *not* be shared with the client, but taken to personal therapy. Freud (1910d, pp. 144–145) wrote,

> We have become aware of the counter transference, which arises in (the analyst) as a result of the patient's influence on his unconscious feelings, and we are almost inclined to insist that he shall recognize this counter transference in himself and, over come it.

Two years later (1912b, pp. 115–116), his thoughts were different, suggesting countertransference should be exploited as a therapeutic tool: "To put it into a formula [the analyst] must turn his unconscious like a receptive organ toward the transmitting unconscious of the patient".

It is perhaps this evoking of our own "stuff" that fascinates me. Sometimes, so much so that one is left asking, does the client get the therapist they need and, indeed, the therapist the client they need? The following vignettes from supervision sessions throw some light on this.

"The ex-partner"

In a recent supervision session, a supervisee reflected about the disturbing similarity of his client to his own personal story, and wanted to look at what had gone on in a recent session.

The client's story of hurt and despair regarding a former partner were parallel to his own, and, as he retold the session, it was clear from his body language, and particularly his breathing, how intense had been the meeting of these two people. His client was stuck, afraid, cowed by the presence of a former partner who had badly treated him, and the sessions were difficult. The client wanted to move on, but, because of the children, the past and presence of this threatening ex-partner were always there. He seemed afraid of his ex-partner and was always apologizing for, or condoning, her behaviour.

In one session, months into their work together, the supervisee turned to his client and said, "I have to share something with you: at this moment I feel full of rage; absolute rage and anger. I am furious at 'her'; I want to tell her to fuck off, leave you alone, and scream can't she see what she has done to you, is doing to you, and how hard it has been for you."

The client nodded, looked his therapist straight in the eyes, and bent his head. For the first time in their sessions together, he cried; tears of anger and rage poured out. Their work continues, but has moved to a different level.

The supervisee in our session was confused; he was aware that he could easily have worded his feeling in the session as "leave *me* alone and can't you see what you have done to *me*". He was confused and worried about what were his and what were his client's affects.

The supervision session was able to explore this and reflect on the importance of both supervision and personal therapy, and recognize the importance of continually reflecting on from where, as therapists, we respond, and the provocation of our own conscious and unconscious that can take place within the therapeutic alliance. As he explored his reaction, he was aware of his own story and aware that, as Freud suggested, his unconscious had picked up the unconscious dialogue of his client's anger at his ex-partner. Through this interaction, the therapist had enabled the client to express what, to date, he had not known: his own rage. The supervisee said that on many earlier occasions he had been tempted to explain to the client that he, too, had had a difficult ex-partner. He saw from this experience that that would not have been helpful or appropriate, but the latest interaction was.

The absent father

In another supervision session, a supervisee brought her concerns regarding a client and the impact she felt his story was having on her.

The client was male, and she had grown very fond of him until he started to explain, weeks into their sessions, that his real reason for coming to therapy was that he was involved in an extra-marital affair and was planning on leaving his wife and three daughters.

The supervisee's own story was one of abandonment by her father when she was young, and, although she herself had had years of personal therapy, she was shocked by her reaction in the session. She had wanted to turn to the client and tell him how her father had left her and how awful it had been and how she hated him, and she said it was all she could do not to tell him. She explained that his revelation had left her feeling betrayed again, as though she had been sucked in by this man, imagining from his talk that he was a good husband and a kind father, the father she had never had. She said it left her doubting her judgement, and she was concerned that her own hurt was too prevalent in the session.

Again, the importance of both supervision and personal therapy were noted, but also, as her work continued with this client, the significance and place countertransference can have in developing the therapeutic process.

Over the following few weeks the supervisee heard, possibly for the first time, another view of a situation she felt she had experienced. She was surprised to hear from her client of his love for his wife, and the difficulty in leaving her and his daughters, whom he adored; of his own turmoil, guilt, and shame; his struggle for years to try to do the right thing and stay in the marriage, and how unhappy both he and his wife were. It was this that they worked with in the following sessions, again highlighting how unhelpful it would have been for the client to be aware of his therapist's own story, but how, somewhere in the unconscious, meeting the therapist's anger met with the client's guilt and shame.

The loss of a child

In another session, a supervisee explained how her client had recently lost a teenage daughter in a traffic accident. The client had asked if she had children. The supervisee was very conscious that not only did she have children, but her own daughter was of a similar age. She felt put on the spot and the thoughts of ignoring or deflecting the question flashed through her mind, but she found herself replying yes.

The sessions were, of course, very emotional, as the client's loss was unbearable. In one session she explained how her daughter had died before hearing examination results, and how she would never take her well-earned place at university. Again, for my supervisee this was extremely difficult, as the client asked her if her children were at university. The supervisee's dilemma was that in her household they were celebrating her daughter's success and preparing for her going off to university. This time, in response to her client's question, she replied that her son was, and that her daughter was going; she was not sure why she had given specific detail in her reply, but felt it impossible to ignore the question, which felt so direct.

Was it helpful for this client to know her therapist had children? Was her client searching for that shared experience of being a mother? At her next session, she brought a copy of a school friend's memory of her daughter, which had been read out at the funeral service. My supervisee was greatly concerned that, on reading this, she had started to cry, consumed by the sadness. She found her client passing her the tissues, aware in that moment of something very special and tender shared between two mothers as well as a client and therapist.

Somehow, it is the collision of the '"meeting" described in the above that fascinates me. If, as I understand, the unconscious is always out there communicating with the "other", while we, as therapists, work with our awareness of this, what of *our unconscious* dialogue with our client's unconscious? In other words, our stuff talking to the client, what happens to this in the process? The small research project I did looking at therapist self-disclosure when something of the client's story touched his or her own story, found a prevalence of anxiety in the therapeutic arena. In many ways, I was charged from the onset of the study not to have preconceived thoughts about any potential findings from the research. However, I was from the onset very interested to reflect on whether I was alone with my own thoughts, concerns, and, indeed, anxiety about self-disclosure, as it always seemed to be a rather taboo subject.

Having found anxiety prevalent around discussion and research on the subject, I wonder, does this anxiety resonate with our clients, are they conscious of this, and does it help or hinder the therapeutic relationship and process? I suppose the debate goes on.

As a final muse on the subject of disclosure, I wonder whether enough is discussed about "us" as relational humans and the impact this has on our work. I am very aware that, on some days, I am more present to my clients than on other days.

What do we do with our own "stuff" that is present, as in "present tense", and undoubtedly present (in the room) in the dynamics of the therapeutic relationship?

Most of us have partners, children, parents, the normal trappings and personal ongoings of life. When parts of our everyday life are more amplified, say, a sick relative, someone close going for an interview, operation, exams (any number of examples can be cited), where does this stuff sit in the therapeutic alliance as we work with our clients? Do we, at times like this, glance more at the clock; what of our body language: does that say something, our eyes, our focus, our interest? At these times, can levels of patience be different? I know that I could answer yes to all of these, which can leave me feeling I am not doing a good enough job.

Personal therapy is undoubtedly crucial, as is supervision and self-awareness, in looking after us. Ideally, on some occasions, we might be best not working, but this could be said for many jobs. We do not want our dentist, doctor, pilot, to name a few, to be distracted . . . or our therapist. Yet, our work is also our living, so we cannot not work when day-to-day interruptions affect us, and were we to, this may well be damaging to our clients, some of who need very boundaried and regular sessions and the security of us being there on a weekly basis.

Holidays are important, but again I muse . . . what about the everyday distracting stuff? I personally try very hard to make my consulting room a room where I work and where I employ a mind-set in which I engage in the other and put aside my stuff. But I would be lying if I said that there are not times when it gets in the way. Do my clients sense this? I do not know. Is it something to address in the room? I do not know. I do not think so, but again I am left pondering about the unconscious dialogue. To date, I rest with the fact that I am thinking about it, aware of it . . . and I will muse on.

Your reflection

- What, I wonder, as this chapter has been read, were your thoughts, if you are a therapist, of your story and where it sits alongside your client work? That special resonance that can take us by surprise in the relatedness of the other's story . . .
- What happens to you in that moment where one person's story taps into yours, what do you do, what do you think, what does your body do? Are there outward signs of a deeper understanding, collusion, and anxiety, and how much do you store and take to supervision and/or personal therapy, and what, if anything, do you share with the client? Does it draw you closer or distance you . . .. the questions are endless!

Recommended readings

Vickers, S. (2007). *The Other Side of You*. London: HarperPerennial.

This is, for me, a special book that, although a novel, relates to the above. A psychotherapist herself, the author somehow, in this novel, portrays a deep, resounding and beautiful meeting of two people.

From a more academic perspective, Patrick Casement's books are invaluable, particularly

Casement, P. (2006). *Learning From Life Becoming a Psychoanalyst*. London: Routledge.

CHAPTER TEN

Concluding reflection

T his book can, as suggested earlier, be seen as an extension of a previous project about reflective practice. It can be read alone, or in connection with the book titled *Reflective Practice in Counselling and Psychotherapy* (Bager-Charleson, 2010). A distinct theme in both these books is that some professions rely, more than others, on "judgements" coloured by personal, cultural, and theoretical values and beliefs. The idea of a distanced, emotionally uninvolved expert equipped with off-the-peg solutions of ready-made knowledge rarely finds its way into the "swampy lowlands of practice mired in confusion and uncertainty" (Taylor, 2008, p. 78). We regard this as relevant when considering both how and why we practise. To us, in our peer group, it makes much more sense to, as Taylor says, consider "the complexities and ambiguities of practice [when] working with patients". We have never found that ready-made, off-the-peg solutions lend themselves to understanding our work. With the exception of authors such as Wosket (2003), Rowan and Jacobs (2002), and others mentioned earlier, we have often missed books that elaborate on this dilemma, the so-called "reflection-in-practice" dilemma. In spite of Freud's early attempts to "make" psychoanalysis into a medical science, there are few, if any "two plus two makes four" rules (Guggenbuhl-Craig, 2009) for when and why people meet in a consultation room. It strikes us as important to "own" one's underlying personal, cultural, and theoretical assumptions and to recognize the impact these may have on how we select and organize the information that we eventually act upon. So, we have brought this kind of thinking with us into the area of *why therapists choose to be therapists* in the fist place.

Reflexive awareness

Reflexivity was addressed in the beginning of the book as a topical theme, and we have considered the issue throughout the book. Reflexivity involves revisiting, re-examining and re-searching one's own motivations and strategies with other options in mind. As Finlay and Gough (2003, p. 5) put it, "[R]esearchers no longer question the need for reflexivity; the question is 'how to do it'?"

This book contributes to the debate about "how to do" reflexivity, both in terms of our own separate narratives about why we choose to practise and also in terms of references to literature and other people's views on the subject. Again, it is surprisingly "quiet" about reflexivity within counselling and psychotherapy, compared to fields such as social work and nursing. Reflexivity embraces the postmodern critique of the industrialized, modern society that so readily puts its faith into universal and scientific "truths". Kvale (1999, p. 32) refers to postmodernity as "characterised by a loss of belief in an objective world". Moving away from the belief in a universal will, general laws, and history of nature, postmodern thinking explores people in their local context. Narratives are often a way of approaching this subject. Loewenthal and Snell (2003) stress the importance of postmodern thinking in psychotherapy. Both myself and Pam have been influenced and inspired by Loewenthal's MSc programme at Roehampton University, where postmodern thinking has a prominent role.

"Local truths" is a theme in all our stories about why we practise. Intercultural, transpersonal, and social constructionist angles are explored by Sherna, Susan, and Sheila when they revisit their motivations for being therapists. Sherna and Sheila both explore how "stories" told on different levels help to shape the way we understand ourselves. Stories about good and bad, right and wrong, appropriate and inappropriate are handed down within and between families and groups defined through geographical, historical, and socio-economic circumstances. As Foucault highlights with his research about *exclusion* and *inclusion* in society, therapists are in a powerful position with regard to the perception of sane and insane, normal and abnormal. Whose interest do we serve? As Sherna illustrated through her experiences in her training, concepts such as "real", "emotionally mature", and "sane" are relative concepts. "When will I be real for you?", wondered Sherna, when her Western, person-centred trainer expressed frustration over Sherna's way of being. The fact that meanings shift over time, as Foucault's post-structuralist research implies, is a warning to us all about embracing diagnoses and labels too "blindly".

The idea proposed in postmodern theory that there are many "local" truths, as opposed to universally sacred beliefs' truths, resonates with what Schön suggests in his concept frame-reflection: there are many different ways in which we can frame our understanding. The issue of power is highlighted through the branch within reflective practice called emancipatory reflection and critical reflexivity (Fook, 2002; Pease & Fook, 1999). Reflective practice "is not a mere quietist navel-gazing", as Bolton (2005, p. 5) puts it. "Reflective practise work can become politically, socially and psychologically useful . . . It supports, demands even, practitioners thinking about values . . . Values which underpin practice are rarely analysed and questioned.

Critical reflective practice (Fook, 2002; Pease & Fook, 1999) takes the idea of local truths further, into the personal realms of the therapist and in the context of socio-cultural, political structures.

Reflexivity involves dialectical engagement based on a back-and-forth interplay of opposing ideas. Different assumptions, ideas, and ways of looking at things are pitted against each other with the purpose of broadening our understanding of the way we position ourselves in our practice. Reflexivity encourages us to "try on" other perspectives and regularly reconsider the impact of our own theoretical, personal, cultural, and political underlying values and beliefs.

Informed practice?

Within theory around evidence-based practice, reflexivity is often discussed as a hindrance, ideally to be eliminated. When defining the phrase "evidence-based practice", Webber refers to "reflexive action" as a contrast, an opposite to the "conscientious, explicit and judicious" practice that evidence-based decisions rely on:

> Evidence-practice is about considered rather than reflexive action. Or, in other words, it requires practitioners to consider evidence before making decisions, rather than acting first and reflecting after the event . . . Evidence-based social care is the conscientious, explicit and judicious use of current best evidence. [2008, p. 3]

Webber highlights the undesirable element in practice based on an "acting first and reflecting afterwards" approach, which actually is compatible with what Schön wants to avoid with reflecting-in practice. Few practitioners and researchers cherish actions based on either non-informed or biased decisions; these are the kind of strategies that Schön proposes that we avoid through systematic frame-reflection. Frame-reflection involves, as illustrated in the case studies earlier, stopping in one's track, raising the question "what am I actually acting upon?" Where does my decision "come from"; where do I *hear* from, on a personal, theoretical/professional, and cultural level?

In this book, several references have been made to theories about the pitfalls in assuming that people in "the helping professions" ought to be "sorted" and able to put their own needs outside "the room". This image of the helper can be a hindrance to owning up to and exploring one's own prejudices, "blind spots", and vulnerabilities. The expectations of the therapist as a "sterile surgeon" will enjoy a renaissance if expectations proposed by, at times, too narrow evidence-based thinking become too unrealistic. To equate evidence-based practice with "not to be influenced by outside pressures" (Webber, 2008, p. 3) could backfire.

In this book, reflexivity and reflective practice have been addressed as ongoing and natural issues to attend to and confront, rather than hope to eliminate. Therapists do not, as Sussman (1992) writes, take much else at face value: why should the therapist's own reasons for working so often be construed in, for instance, "altruistic terms"? Why should we not expect to go a bit deeper than that? What could be "shameful" or inappropriate for therapists to need to "confront their shadow again and again", as Guggenbuhl-Craig proposes?

Evidenced-based practice is, write Knott and Scragg (2008, p. 8) "scientifically informed"; it "relies on rational knowledge to inform practice that has been tested through scientific methods". Evidence-based data usually rely on statistics to "evidence" practice. We have found statistics limited in gaining insight into the rationales and motivations for being a therapist. Quantitative data and statistics have thrown interesting light on the distribution of motivations within the therapeutic community. Statistics bring issues to the surface, facts stare us, so to speak, in the face. As an academic adviser, I entered this project with a hypothesis in mind. Hypothetically, I expected "interest in people" to be a dominating, or, at least, competitive, reply. The statistics present a different picture. Yet, from those in the survey who elaborated on their answers, the replies oozed, to my mind, curiosity and openness to the possibility that everything has got many angles and is usually construed with previous experience in mind. This seemed also to be the general idea proposed, not only in my own personal story, but in those of my colleagues. Our own stories become, in this light, case studies, illustrating the different categories. They highlight what can happen to quantitative data when moving into the qualitative domain; "childhood" and "adult life crisis" invariably become ambiguous and complex areas. as they are in the "swampy lowlands" of real life.

The evidence-based practice debate can easily become polarized into quantitative *vs.* qualitative "camps". It is, perhaps, more constructive to explore how the two approaches may overlap and complement each other. Although reflective practice distances itself from the natural scientific, traditional definition of "objective", the two approaches certainly meet around an interest in "informed" practice as opposed to non-reflected, instinctive, or habitual strategy. Davies (2007) offers a definition of evidence-based practice, which highlights that practice ought to be communicated and verified by others: "The unifying theme in all definitions is that evidence (however construed) can be independently observed and verified, and that there is a broad consensus as to its contents (if not its interpretation)".

Reflective writing

In this book, reflective *writing* is addressed as a form of reflective practice. We regard writing as "a vehicle for reflection", as Bolton (2005) puts it: "We do not store experience as data, we 'story' it . . . Stories are the mode we use to make sense of ourselves and our world".

The "relative permanence" (Smith, 1985) in writing permits us to linger with our own way of construing "reality". Bolton compares it with a film: "[In writing] you can freeze the film; reflect upon one frame or a short series, then run the film backward and review previous scene in the light of reflection upon a later one".

This outlook has guided our own thinking about motivations for practising as therapists. The book has grown into an enquiry that can be compared with "practice-based research", although we prefer to call it re-search.

Re-searching motivations for being a therapist

This project originated in private queries and discussions. For me, it was triggered by the article that Susan brought with her to one of our meetings. The project ignited easily; it tapped into something already there—we just needed the right impetus.

The project has developed into a piece of "practice based inquiry". Du Plock (2010) asserts that research happens more often than the traditional scientific definition of the terms admits to. Du Plock refers to research as a dialectic process that moves between naïve and systematic enquiry. The "naïve" enquiry is an inevitable aspect of research;

> The word "research" itself can feel intimidating: if you are not a graduate then you may believe (erroneously I think) that you are a stranger to research; if you have an arts degree you may feel estranged from the sorts of "scientific" research increasingly

required in the therapy field . . . We get into difficulties, it seems to me, when we . . . begin to see research as something different and separate from that with which we are already intimately involved . . . [p. 112]

The systematic element of research and enquiry can, as Barber (2006) suggests, be described as an "ongoing debate". What else is written, said, and thought in the area? Du Plock continues, "Research must not, of course, remain only of personal significance if it is to have any impact on professional practice—it must be disseminated, and evaluated by our peers, colleagues, and clients" (*ibid.*)

We do not regard our enquiry as research, as such. We do, however, consider it as re-search. The term "re-searching" captures how writing about an area of our practice in this way invariably expands one's understanding and outlook. We return to something familiar, at times taken for granted, with new eyes, not only because of our own individual reflections, but, perhaps primarily, in light of the dialectical process involved in reading each other's texts, giving and receiving and continuing writing with colleagues' other perspectives in mind. An important part of this re-search has been to put our own query into a larger context. What do other therapists think? And what has been written about the subject already?

The outcome of the enquiry

What have we learnt about therapists' motivations for being therapists? Perhaps, more than anything, this re-search has raised new questions. Why is it, for instance, such a seemingly 'hushed-up" area?

The literature about why therapists choose to be therapists is, as suggested, limited. The reasons end up sounding either very "bad" or extremely rewarding and "good". There are, in other words, signs of a curious division or "split" between "good" and "bad" therapists. This split between something wholly good or only bad is unusual construct for psychotherapy to work from; it is normally something we aim to challenge and reconstruct. Yet, it seems to us to be a surprisingly uncontested notion in the context of therapists' own motivations. It is likely that this split reflects a lack of dialogue between practitioners. It can be linked to the absence of the kind of dialectic engagements that secures opposite viewpoints to meet, as addressed earlier. McLeod contends that counsellors and psychotherapists are more reluctant than others to engage in research, debate, and writing about their practice. One difficult aspect of developing practice research appears to stem from a reported sense of "betrayal" towards the clients (see McLeod, 1999). Sometimes, the very notion of approaching a therapeutic experience with a complementary research interest is construed as a distancing, emotionless, and exploiting action.

Kottler (1993) and Sussman (1992), however, link this "silence" to the tendency to idealize the therapist, again in line with the "splitting" of all "weak" bits from the therapist. She is "strong" and "sorted" in the eyes of both the public and among peers.

We are not disputing that these two types of motivation exist, but find it more likely that they exist side by side; we are all good *and* bad, as we are quick to tell our clients. It seems reasonable to suspect that polarizing motivations will silence, name and shame, rather than encourage the reflexive awareness which is nourished by "trying on" opposing perspectives.

Behind our question "why" has developed an interest in how therapists think, reason, and make sense of their profession. It certainly seems natural that the answer to the question "why practise as a therapist" seems to undergo constant transformation in light of new experiences and connections. In our survey, many therapists referred to a combination of factors. The therapists who elaborated on their chosen category of reasons approached the question "why" as a multi-layered issue. The therapists have made sense of their interest, connected their original experience with new, sometimes "foreign" perspectives, which have caused them to reconsider and "transform" (Roffey-Barentsen & Malthouse, 2009) their assumptions about themselves and their world. This was also highlighted in our different case studies, our "stories". In her example with Amy, Susan illustrates, for instance, how suddenly feeling lost and sad herself during a session developed into a learning experience, with new light thrown on to her own motives for practising. These kind of reflection-in-practice experiences are ongoing matters. They are referred to here as both inevitable and potentially useful. Susan refers to a situation where she is "thinking on her feet" at the same time as she brings fragments of knowledge into play while building theories and responses that fit the new situation. Susan's own strategy develops also, perhaps most importantly, in the context of "back talk" (Schön, 1983, p. 347) with her client. Schön (*ibid.*, p. 68) writes,

> The practitioner allow himself to experience surprise, puzzlement, or confusion in a situation which he finds uncertain or unique. He reflects on the phenomenon before him, and on the prior understandings which have been implicit in his behavior. He carries out an experiment which serves to generate both a new understanding of the phenomenon and a change in the situation.

Susan has spent time reflecting on her reactions earlier, but this reflective writing experience offered her, as well as the others in the group, the option of reviewing events systematically. She reconnected in a new way with her motives for practising as a therapist, in a similar way to myself and, for instance, to Francesca, through a client who triggered particular issues in her. In both Susan's and Sherna's case, the reflection-on-action has resulted in additional sections about the therapist's use of self in their respective modalities, which are transpersonal and intercultural therapy, respectively. The reflective writing has both offered and demanded the challenge to consider what we preach through our modality. We have, in other words, had to critically review the relationship between our espoused theory and our theory-in-use.

Reflective practice is a dialogical and dialectical affair. It is a process where old meanings are reconstructed through an engagement in oppositional perspectives and by adopting new and "foreign" angles. Discussions and ongoing feedback are essential aspects in reflective practice and reflexive awareness. Bolton (2005, p. 4) writes,

> Effective reflective practice and reflexivity meet the paradoxical need both to tell and retell our stories in order to feel secure enough, and yet critically examine our actions and those of others, in order dynamically to increase our understanding of ourselves and our practice.

We have aimed to share some of our own experiences, and we encourage you to explore for yourself the benefits of reflective writing in the company of "critical friends". To review, research, discuss, and obtain ongoing feedback from peers and colleagues is approached as important for the well-being of both the therapists and their clients. We use, as addressed, research in a broad sense, with an emphasis on revisiting, re-searching, our professional involvement. Enquiry is a better word. Our variation of what Heron (1998) and Reason (1994) refer to as collaborative or "co-operative" enquiry illustrates the underlying ethos for this book, which is that it is also good for therapists "to talk" and to engage dialogically and dialectically with, at times, oppositional stances.

Our last point of reflection mirrors the task which we set ourselves, with this book as its subsequent outcome. We invite you to share the satisfaction of re-searching and replenishing your own practice.

Your reflection

- Who would you feel comfortable writing and "creating" together with?
- What would you like to explore further? What niggles, or perhaps seriously bothers, you with regard to your practice?
- Would reflective writing work for you? Do you find it easier to express yourself through painting, clay, or other "creative" means?
- Discuss the idea with peers and *invite* to a regular group.

We hope that you will enjoy your professional role as valued listener, and as someone who has got something to say.

We look forward to hearing about your practice!

REFERENCES

Aldridge, J., & Becker, S. (2003). *Children Caring for Parents with Mental Illness*. Portland: Policy Press.

Alvesson, M., & Skoldeberg, K. (2000). *Reflexive Methodology*. London: Sage.

Argyris, M., & Schön, D. (1974). *Theory In Practice: Increasing Professional Effectiveness*. San Francisco, CA: Jossey-Bass.

Argyris, C., & Schön, D. (1978). *Organizational Learning: A Theory of Action Perspective*. Reading, MA: Addison Wesley.

Auvil, C. A., & Silver, B. W. (1984). Therapist self disclosure: when is it appropriate? *Perspectives in Psychiatric Care, 22*: 57–61.

Bager-Charleson, S. (2010). *Reflective Practice in Counselling and Psychotherapy*. Exeter: Learning Matters.

Banister, P., Burman, E., Parker, I., Taylor, M., & Tindall, C. (1994). *Qualitative Methods in Psychology; A Research Guide*. Buckingham: Open University Press.

Barber, P. (2006). *Becoming a Practitioner Researcher. A Gestalt Approach to Holistic Inquiry*. London: Middlesex University Press.

Bateman, A., & Holmes, J. (1999). *Introduction to Psychoanalysis— Contemporary Theory and Practice*. London: Brunner Routledge.

Billig, M. (1997). Freud and Dora: repressing an oppressed identity. *Theory, Culture and Society, 14*: 29–55.

Bion, W. (1962). *Learning From Experience*. London: Karnac.

Bolton, G. (2005). *Reflective Practice: Writing and Professional Development*. London: Sage.

Bolton, G., Field, V., & Thompson, K. (Eds) (2006). *Writing Works: A Resource Handbook for Therapeutic Writing Workshops and Activities*. London & Philadelphia: Jessica Kingsley Publishers.

Bridges, N. A. (2001). Therapist's self disclosure: expanding the comfort zone. *Psychotherapy: Theory, Research, Practice, Training*, 38(1): 21–30.

Broden, M. (2005). Developmental theories in the process of change. In: I. Nolan & P. Nolan (Eds.), *Object Relations & Integrative Psychotherapy* (pp. 80–96). London: Whurr.

Brown, L. S., & Walker, L. E. (1990). Feminist therapy perspectives on self disclosure. In: G. Stricker & M. Fisher (Eds.), *Self-disclosure in the Therapeutic Relationship* (pp. 135–156). New York: Plenum.

Buber, M. (1946). *Between Man and Man*. Glasgow: Fontana Library, 1971.

Cardinal, D., Hayward, J., & Jones, G. (2005). *Epistemology: The Theory of Knowledge*. London: Hodder Murray.

Carter, D., & Gradin, S. (2001). *Writing as Reflective Action. A Reader*. New York: Longman.

Casement, P. (2002). *Learning From Our Mistakes*. New York & London: Brunner-Routledge.

Casement, P. (2008a). *Learning from Life—Becoming a Psychoanalyst*. London: Routledge.

Casement, P. (2008b). *Learning From Our Mistakes—Beyond Dogma in Psychoanalysis and Psychotherapy*. New York: Psychology Press.

Cashdan, S. (1988). *Object Relation Therapy—Using the Relationship*. Ontario: Penguin.

Chernin, K. (1986). *The Hungry Self. Women, Eating and Identity*. New York: Harper Perennial.

Chernin, K (1991). The underside of the mother–-daughter relationship. In: C. Zweig & J. Abrams (Eds.), *Meeting the Shadow. The Hidden Power of the Dark Side of Human Nature* (pp. 54–58). New York: Penguin.

Clarkson, P. (2002). *The Therapeutic Relationship in Psychoanalysis, Counselling Psychology and Psychotherapy*. London: Whurr.

Cleavely, E. (1993). Relationships: interaction, defences and transformation. In: S. Ruszczynski (Ed.), *Psychotherapy With Couples: Theory and Practice at the Tavistock Institute of Marital Studies* (pp. 55–69). London: Karnac.

Critchley, P. (2006). What, if anything, might you share with your client if something about their story touches your own? Dissertation for the Master of Science Degree in Counselling and Psychotherapy as a Means to Health, Roehampton University.

Davies, M. (2007). *Boundaries in Counselling and Psychotherapy*. Twickenham: Athena Press.

Despenser, S. (2007). Risk assessment: the personal safety of the counselor. *Therapy Today*, March: 12–13.

du Plock, S. (2010). The vulnerable researcher: harnessing reflexivity for practice-based qualitative inquiry. In: S. Bager-Charleson, *Reflective Practice in Counselling and Psychotherapy* (pp. 121–135). Exeter: Learning Matters.

Etherington, K. (2004). *Becoming a Reflexive Researcher: Using Our Selves in Research*. London: Jessica Kingsley.

Erikson, E. (1993). *Young Man Luther: A Study in Psychoanalysis and History*. New York: Norton.

Feltham, C. (Ed.) (1999). *Understanding the Counselling Relationship*. London: Sage.

Finlay, L., & Gough, B. (2003). *Reflexivity: A Practical Guide*. London: Blackwell.

Fook, J. (2002). *Social Work: Critical Theory and Practice*. London: Sage.

Foucault, J. (1984). The birth of the asylum. In: *Madness and Civilisation: A History of Insanity in the Age of Reason*. In: P. Rabinow (Ed.), *The Foucault Reader. The Introduction to Foucault's Thoughts* (pp. 141–168). London: Penguin.

Friedman, M. (1999). *The Worlds of Existentialism*. New Jersey: Humanity Books.

Freud, S. (1910d). The future prospects of psycho-analytic therapy. *S.E.*, *11*: 139–51. London: Hogarth.

Freud, S. (1912b). The dynamics of transference. *S.E.*, *12*: 97–108. London: Hogarth.

Freud, S. (1937). Analysis terminable and interminable. *S.E.*, *23*: 216–253. London, Hogarth, 1964.

Fromm, E. (1998). About the therapeutic relationship. In: I. Rabonowitz (Ed.), *Inside Therapy—Illuminating Writings About Therapists, Patients and Psychotherapy* (pp. 255–265). New York: St Martin's Press.

Gergen, K. (2009). *An Invitation to Social Constructionism* (2nd edn). New York: Sage.

Ghaemi, S. N. (2007). *The Concepts of Psychiatry; A Pluralistic Approach to the Mind and Mental Illness*. Baltimore, MD: Johns Hopkins University Press.

Goldstein, E. G. (1994). Self disclosure in treatment: what therapists do and don't talk about. *Clinical Social Work Journal, 22*: 417–433.

Greenberg, L. R. (1990). Self disclosure in psychotherapy: working with older adults. In: G. Stricker & M. Fisher (Eds.), *Self Disclosure in the Therapeutic Relationship* (pp. 175–190). New York: Plenum.

Guggenbuhl-Craig, A. (1991). Quacks, charlatans, and false prophets. In: C. Sweig & J. Abrams (Eds.), *Meeting the Shadow: Hidden Power of the Dark Side of Human Nature* (pp. 110–115). New York: Penguin.

Guggenbuhl-Craig, A. (2009). *Power in the Helping Professions*. New York: Canada: Spring.

Habermas, J. (1987). *The Theory of Communicative Action*. Boston: Beacon Press.

Hanson, J. (2003). Coming out: therapist self disclosure as a therapeutic technique, with specific application to sexual minority populations. *Canadian Counsellor, 15*: 175–179.

Hawkins, P., & Shohet, S. (2006). *Supervision in the Helping Professions*. Maidenhead: Open University Press.

Heron, J. (1998). *Co-operative Inquiry: Research Into the Human Condition*. London: Sage.

Hill, C. A., & Knox, S. (2001). Self disclosure. *Psychotherapy: Theory Research Practice Training, 38*(4): 413–417.

Jacobs, T. (1999). The question of self disclosure by the analyst: error or advance in technique? *Psychoanalytic Quarterly, 68*(2): 159–183.

Kakar, S. (1978). *The Inner World. Psychoanalytic Study of Childhood and Society in India*. Oxford: Oxford University Press.

Kant, I. (2007) [1781]. *Critique of Pure Reason*. London: Penguin Classics [revised edition].

Knott, C., & Scragg, T. (2008). *Reflective Practice in Social Work*. Hove: Learning Matters.

Knox, S., Hess, S. A., Peterson, D. A., & Hill, C. A. (1997). A qualitative analysis of client perceptions of the effects of helpful therapist self disclosure in long term therapy. *Journal of Counselling Psychology, 44*: 274–283.

Kottler, J. A. (1993). *On Being a Therapist*. San Francisco: Josey-Bass Publishers.

Kvale, S. (Ed.) (1999). *Psychology and Postmodernism*. London: Sage.

Lehman, J. (2008). Telling stories . . . and the pursuit of critical reflection. In: S. White, J. Fook & F. Gardner (Eds), *Critical Reflection in Health and Social Care*. Maidenhead: Open University Press.

Loewenthal, D., & Snell, R. (2003). *Post-modernism for Psychotherapists*. Hove: Brunner & Routledge.

McLeod, J. (1999). *Practitioner Research in Counselling*. London: Sage.

McLeod, J. (2003). *Doing Counselling Research*. London: Sage.

McNamee, S., & Gergen, K. J. (Eds) (1992). *Therapy as a Social Construction*. London: Sage.

Merleau-Ponty, M. (1999). The phenomenology of perception. In: M. Friedman (Ed.), *The Worlds of Existentialism: A Critical Reader*. New York: Humanities Books.

Miller, A. (1997). *The Drama of the Gifted Child—The Search for the True Self*. New York: Basic Books.

Mitchell, J. (2002). *Psychoanalysis and Feminism*. London: Penguin.

Nelson, J. (1991). *Healing The Split*. New York: State University of New York Press.

Nilsson, D. E., Strassberg, D. S., & Bannon, J. (1979). Perceptions of counsellor self disclosure: an analogue study. *Journal of Counselling Psychology, 26*: 399–404.

Nobus, D. (2000). *Jaques Lacan and the Freudian Practice of Psychoanalysis*. London: Taylor & Francis.

Page, S. (1999). *The Shadow and the Counsellor*. London: Routledge.

Papouchis, N. (1990). Self disclosure with children and adolescents. In: G. Stricker & M. Fisher (Eds.), *Self Disclosure In The Therapeutic Relationship* (pp. 157–174). New York: Plenum.

Parker, I. (1994). Qualitative research. In: P. Banister, E. Burman, I. Parker, M. Taylor & C. Tindall (Eds), *Qualitative Methods in Psychology: A Research Guide*. Buckingham: Open University Press.

Parker, I. (2004). *Qualitative Psychology; Introducing Radical Research*. New York: Open University Press.

Pearce, W. B. (1976). The co-ordinated management of meaning; a rules-based. theory of interpersonal communication. In: G. Miller (Ed.), *Explorations in Interpersonal Communication* (pp. 17–36). Beverley Hills: CA: Sage.

Pearce, W. B. (1994). *Interpersonal Communication. Making Social Worlds*. New York: HarperCollins.

Pease, B., & Fook, J. (Eds) (1999). *Transforming Social Work Practice. Postmodern Critical Perspectives*. London & New York: Routledge.

Peck, S. (1993). *Further Along The Road Less Travelled*. London: Simon & Schuster Ltd.

Peterson, Z. D. (2002). More than a mirror: the ethics of therapist self disclosure. *Psychotherapy: Theory, Research, Practice, Training, 39*: 21–31.

Polkinghorne, D. (1988). *Narrative Knowing and the Human Sciences*. Albany, NY: State University of New York Press.

Racker, H. (2001). *Transference and Countertransference*. London: Karnac.

Reason, P. (Ed.) (1994). *Participation in Human Inquiry*. London: Sage.

Roffey-Barentsen, J., & Malthouse, R. (2009). *Reflective Practice in the Lifelong Learning Sector*. Exeter: Learning Matters.

Rogers, C. (1951). *Client Centred Therapy*. London: Constable.

Rogers, C. (1961). *A Therapist's View of Psychotherapy*. London: Constable.

Rogers, C. (1995). *A Way of Being*. New York: Houghton Mifflin.

Roland, S. (1989). *In Search of Self in India and Japan Towards a Cross Cultural Psychology*. New Jersey: Princeton University Press.

Rosen, H., & Kuehlwein, K. (Eds.) (1996). *Constructing Realities*. Boston: Jossey-Bass.

Rowan, J., & Jacobs, M. (2002). *The Therapist's Use of Self*. Buckingham: Open University Press.

Safran, J. D., & Muran, J. C. (1994). Toward a working alliance between research and practice. In: P. F. Talley, H. H. Strupp, & S. F. Butler (Eds.), *Psychotherapy Research and Practice: Bridging the Gap* (pp. 206–226). New York: Basic Books.

Safran, J. D., & Muran, J. C. (2003). *Negotiating the Therapeutic Alliance: A Relational Treatment Guide*. New York: Guilford Press.

Schön, D. A. (1983). *The Reflective Practitioner: How Professionals Think in Action*. New York: Basic Books.

Schön, D., & Rein, M. (1994). *Frame Reflection: Toward the Resolution of Intractable Policy Controversies*. New York: Basic Books.

Schore, A. N. (2008). The human unconscious: the development of the right brain and its role in early emotional life. In: V. Green (Ed.), *Emotional Development in Psychoanalysis, Attachment Theory and Neuroscience* (pp. 23–55). New York: Routledge.

Sedgwick, D. (2005). *The Wounded Healer—Countertransference from a Jungian Perspective*. London: Routledge.

Simi, N. L., & Mahalik, J. R. (1997). Comparison of feminist versus psychoanalytic/dynamic and other therapists on self disclosure. *Psychology of Women Quarterly, 21*: 465–483.

Simon, J. C. (1998). Criteria for therapist self disclosure. *American Journal of Psychotherapy, 62*: 404–415.

Skovholt, T. M., & Ronnestad, M. H. (1995). *The Evolving Professional Self: Stages and Themes in Therapist and Counselor Development*. New York: Wiley.

Skovholt, T. M., & Ronnestad, M. H. (2003). The hope and promise of career life-span counselor and therapist development. *Journal of Career Development, 30*: 1–3.

Smith, F. (1985). *Writing and the Write*. London: Heinemann Educational Books.

Stern, D. N. (2004). *The Present Moment in Psychotherapy and Everyday Life*. New York: Norton.

Storr, A. (1979). *The Art of Psychotherapy*. London: Secker & Warburg.

Strean, H. S. (1998a). "Who listens?" The woman who refused to talk. In: I. Rabonowitz (Ed.), *Inside Therapy—Illuminating Writings About Therapists, Patients and Psychotherapy* (pp. 1–21). New York: St Martin's Press.

Strean, H. S. (1998b). Sometimes I feel like a dirty old man: the woman who tried to seduce me. In: I. Rabonowitz (Ed.), *Inside Therapy — Illuminating Writings About Therapists, Patients and Psychotherapy* (pp. 116–131). New York: St Martin's Press.

Sussman, M. B. (1992). *A Curious Calling—Unconscious Motivations for Practicing Psychotherapy*. New York: Jason Aronson.

Symington, N. (1986). *The Analytic Experience—Lectures from the Tavistock*. London: Free Association Books.

Taylor, B. (2006). *Reflective Practice: A Guide for Nurses and Midwives*. Maidenhead: Open University Press.

Taylor, C. (2008). Practising reflexivity: narrative, reflection and the moral order. In: S. White, J. Fook, & F. Gardner (Eds.), *Critical Reflection in Health and Social Care*. Maidenhead: Open University Press.

van Deurzen, E. (2002). *Existential Counselling and Psychotherapy in Practice*. London: Sage.

Viscott, D. S. (1998). The making of a psychiatrist. In: I. Rabonowitz (Ed.), *Inside Therapy—Illuminating Writings About Therapists, Patients and Psychotherapy* (pp. 32–53). New York: St Martin's Press.

Walsh, N. D. (1996). *Conversations with God*. New Jersey: Putnam.

Watchel, P. L. (1993). *Therapeutic Communication: Principles and Effective Practice*. New York: Guilford Press.

Weaver, M. (2008). Constructivism: some subjective thoughts in a rational world. *The Psychotherapist, Spring*: 1.

Webber, M. (2008). *Evidence-based Policy and Practice in Mental Health Social Work*. Exeter: Learning Matters.

Weinberg, G. (1998). The therapist personality. In: I. Rabonowitz (Ed.), *Inside Therapy—Illuminating Writings About Therapists, Patients and Psychotherapy* (pp. 22–31). New York: St Martin's Press.

Weiner, M. F. (1983). *Therapist Disclosure: The Use of Self in Psychotherapy* (2nd edn). Baltimore: University Park Press.

Wells, T. L. (1994). Therapist self disclosure: its effects on clients and the treatment relationship. *Smith College Studies in Social Work, 65*: 23–41.

White, S., Fook, J., & Gardner, F. (2008). *Critical Reflection in Health and Social Care*. Maidenhead: Open University Press.

Winnicott, D. W. (1974). Fear of breakdown. *International Review of Psychoanalysis, 1*: 103–107.

Winter, R., Buck, A., & Sobieschowska, P. (1999). *Professional Experience & The Investigative Imagination: The Art of Reflective Writing*. London: Routledge.

Wosket, V. (2003). *The Therapeutic Use of Self: Counselling Practice, Research and Supervision*. Hove: Brunner-Routledge.

Yalom, I. D. (1980). *Existential Psychotherapy*. New York: Basic Books.

INDEX